The GREATEST RISK *of* ALL

BOOKS BY WALTER ANDERSON

Courage Is a Three-Letter Word
The Greatest Risk of All

The
GREATEST
RISK *of* ALL

Walter Anderson

A Marc Jaffe Book

HOUGHTON MIFFLIN COMPANY

BOSTON 1988

For information about permission to reproduce selections from
this book, write to Permissions, Houghton Mifflin Company,
2 Park Street, Boston, Massachusetts 02108.

Library of Congress Cataloging-in-Publication Data

Anderson, Walter
The greatest risk of all.

"A Marc Jaffe book."
1. Risk-taking (Psychology)   2. Security
(Psychology)   3. Self-actualization (Psychology)
4. Anderson, Walter, date.   5. Celebrities—
United States—Interviews.   6. Celebrities—United
States—Psychology.   I. Title.
BF637.R57A53   1988   158'.1   88-9265
ISBN 0-395-46516-8

Printed in the United States of America

Q 10 9 8 7 6 5 4 3 2 1

For
SCOTT MEREDITH
who encouraged me to take a risk

We should be careful to get out of an experience only the wisdom that is in it — and stop there; lest we be like the cat that sits down on a hot-stove lid. She will never sit down on a hot-stove lid again, and that is well; but also she will never sit down on a cold one any more.

— MARK TWAIN

Imagine standing on one side of a rising drawbridge. If we hurry, we can leap across the widening gap, but a friend slows us, warning, "Look how far you could fall."

"But if we don't cross this bridge," we say, "we're stuck here — and this is not where we want to be."

"Maybe you should wait," our friend suggests, "until it's safer."

"But if we don't go *now*," we explain, "we'll miss out."

"Look!" squeals our friend, gesturing frantically at the opening, now even larger.

"We're wasting time," we tell each other. "C'mon, it's easy."

Is it?

The
GREATEST
RISK *of* ALL

Introduction

I thought I knew where to begin. *Risk*. I'd just look up the word. Well, trying to find a really good definition of risk, I discovered, is like hunting along a sandy beach for a one-carat diamond. Every grain may have the look, but none has the substance. Every definition I read was depressing, packed with words like *danger, hazard, peril, jeopardy, exposure, chance of injury, damage,* and *loss*. It's not surprising, it became clear to me, why risk-taking makes us so anxious. After all, haven't we heard all our lives that we should avoid danger, hazards, and peril?

Yet to find true security, to be confident, to know real love, to be fulfilled, to be at peace with ourselves and others, we must learn to take risks. There's no other way. Our lives improve only when we take chances — and the first and most difficult risk we can take is to be honest with ourselves. Have you ever asked, do I need a change? I have, and simply asking the question, I've found, is in itself taking a risk. If I answer yes, I must act — or be frustrated.

Do *you* need a change?

I've written this book to help you answer this question — to help you explore your opportunities, to help you understand what happens when you actually take a risk, anticipate and respond to the kind of doubts that emerge every time you reach for a goal larger than any you've achieved before. The honest accounts of personal discovery that follow embrace the theme, the deeply held conviction, that we can learn to take risks. The people I've interviewed are identified, despite the intimate nature of their stories, and some you will undoubtedly recognize as famous leaders in their fields. My own story of discovery is here too. Together we will probe provocative questions, exploring some subjects that even the closest of friends find risky to discuss. We will examine how we define risks throughout life — as children, as adolescents, as adults — and we will explore the dynamic factors, the three losses common to every risk.

Do you want greater love, esteem, power, security?

Do I need a change?

Clearly, taking a risk is difficult — and danger is a vital part of risk-taking. To risk is to stretch further than we have before.

What stops us?

What stops *me?*

Like so many others, I was taught how *not* to take a risk — as if risk can be postponed! Yet risk is inescapable. Hasn't each of us faced a first day of school, the possibility of a new job, a move, the gain or loss of friends, relatives, lovers? Hasn't each of us, particularly as we've grown older, avoided some opportunity because we resisted being seen as a beginner, an amateur?

What are we most afraid of?

I don't want to be embarrassed.

The perfectly natural fear of humiliation rises in any normal human being faced with important choices. Yet just as our concern about being embarrassed can inhibit risk-taking, so can it inspire us. Fear of humiliation is so overwhelming when we're teenagers, for example, that it often prompts us to be the greatest, though not necessarily the wisest, risk-takers: *I dare you!* Even as mature adults, though, aren't there times when we're willing to take chances to avoid looking foolish?

Such apparently contradictory phenomena intrigued me as I started my research. Why, I wondered, do I have such a difficult time remembering risks that failed? Which do I regret more, risks I've taken or risks I've avoided? Why, when faced with two ways to gain something of value, do I tend to pick the safer alternative, but when faced with two ways to avoid losses, do I tend to pick the riskier alternative? Can I learn to reduce the nervousness I feel when facing risks?

Nowhere in these pages will risk-taking be made to seem easy; it's too important a process to be trivialized. Neither will you be encouraged to take a risk that is hazardous or that does not fulfill a real need. We're not going to study skydivers, tightrope walkers, or young Marines rappelling down a cliff. This book is about the necessary risks we face throughout our lives, from birth to our final moments — the growing and changing we must experience unless we are to live, as Theodore Roosevelt suggested, "in the gray twilight that knows not victory or defeat."

I'm sure, as you turn these pages, you will hear my voice in a way quite unlike that of anyone else. This book, after all, is meant to be personal — and the stories written here are intimate. They're about people like you and me finding ourselves, finding our *dreams*.

I have learned to be a risk-taker. You can too.

Part One

WE'RE ALL MAGICIANS. Each of us has a great bag of tricks that we add to every day of our lives. Not surprisingly, when we're unsure of what to do, we dig deep for the magic that has worked before. In the next several pages we're going to examine these tricks — how we've learned from our earliest years to hesitate, to be cautious, sometimes to behave like a child when we most need to be adult, how and why we cling to false notions that cripple our ability to take risks, and, most important, how to shake ourselves free.

Let's begin by asking, what does a child learn?

A child learns to trust.

No lesson of youth is more meaningful. In our very first moments we feel sensations, pleasant and unpleasant — but all is a blur. Then, gradually, a sorting out occurs. We learn we are not the crib that holds us, the blanket that warms us. Sometime during infancy we make perhaps the most remarkable discovery of all: We are not the hand that feeds us. *I* and *you*, we find, are not the same — and we realize we need *you*. We must trust *you*.

The quality of the relationship between *you* and *I* flavors the relationships that follow. We learn what we can control; we learn whom we can trust; and by taking risks, we start to develop our personalities. Other people, by responding to these efforts of ours, help us to measure our progress. We ask, how good am I?

It may seem incredibly obvious to a grownup that trusting another human being can be a great risk. How, though, have we come to this understanding? Like me, you've learned from your experience, beginning in childhood. We're never more vulnerable than when we trust someone — but, paradoxically, if we cannot trust, neither can we find love or joy.

How do we know these things? Where and what is our foundation?

A child learns to trust.

My earliest memory of a lesson in trust — a painful story about a truly reckless risk — involves an event that occurred when I was eleven, when I risked my life for a two-dollar piece of jewelry.

It was 1955, a Monday in October, as I paused outside a novelty shop, one of dozens in Times Square. I glanced down at the new silver-plated identification bracelet on my left wrist, and I smiled.

A day earlier a friend and I had taken the subway from 241st Street in the Bronx to the heart of Manhattan. We had been window-shopping when I spotted the identification bracelet.

"Look at that," I said. "Only two bucks."

"You gonna buy it?" my friend asked.

"I don't know."

"They engrave it free."

"Yeah," I said, "but if I spend my money now, I'll have nothing left — and it's early."

He nodded.

Later, riding the subway back to 241st Street, I knew I had made a mistake: I *had* to have that bracelet.

"How are you gonna get it?" my friend asked, warning, "We got school tomorrow."

"I have a plan," I told him.

So, walking through Times Square at noon the following day, the new identification bracelet secure on my wrist, I was more than a little pleased with myself and my plan.

Only a couple of hours earlier I had been sitting in my fifth-grade class at Immanuel Lutheran School in Mount Vernon, New York. Then I had faked an illness — faked it so well I was driven home by the principal's wife.

"Are your parents here?" she had asked me as she brought her car to a stop on the other side of Mount Vernon, in front of the four-story tenement at the corner of Eleventh Avenue and Third Street.

"My grandmother is," I said, which was true.

"What floor is yours?"

"The second."

"All right," she said, "but wave from your window, so I know you're inside."

I'm stuck now, I thought.

"Okay?" she asked.

"Okay," I said.

I slowly, unhappily, walked through the entrance of the apartment building, then I began to trudge up the first flight of stairs. Before I reached the top step, though, my mood improved; I had an idea. My family lived in a four-room rail-road flat, its living room windows facing Eleventh Avenue. I stopped in front of our door. Down the hallway in which I stood was another window, next to those in our apartment.

I looked to my right, paused, then made my decision. I scooted down the hallway, opened the window, waved, and stepped back. I held my breath. Would she leave?

Finally, when I couldn't stand it any longer, only seconds I'm sure, I leaned back to the window and peeked.

Her car was gone.

Now, I told myself, I'll get that bracelet.

The trick was to return home from Manhattan, new identification bracelet stuffed in my pocket, before the time I normally would have arrived from school. I silently rehearsed the lines I knew I'd need with my grandmother.

"Grandma," I'd begin, "they sent me home early because I didn't feel well . . ."

Naturally, she'd send me to bed, and later, when my mother came home, Grandma would tell her that I was sick. My mother, I was sure, would write the note I'd need to return to school the following day — and no doubt she'd thank the principal's wife for driving me.

All's well that ends well, I thought.

Of course, if I were to arrive home on time or late, I'd be in trouble, big trouble. That possibility didn't worry me until I left the novelty store, walked to the subway in Times Square, and suddenly found myself confused amid a crush of people. Which train? Which track?

"Mister," I spoke through a grille to a man in an enclosed token booth, "which train do I take to get to 241st Street and White Plains Road in the Bronx?"

He pointed to a stairwell, then shouted, "Remember to change trains at 180th Street!"

Almost as he spoke, a construction worker in heavy tan workboots, wearing a faded denim shirt and jeans, tapped my elbow, surprising me. He said, "Here, I'll show you. I'm going the same way."

I was uneasy.

He was a man of scars — his cheeks were crisscrossed with tiny jagged scars, his eyebrows were scarred in ragged sections, his ears were cauliflowered, and he had a large scar across the bridge of his flattened nose and another slicing both his upper and lower lips.

"I'm a fighter," he said as he followed me into a crowded subway car.

I nodded.

He was sandy-haired, probably in his mid-thirties, and I could see the muscles of his arms flexing through his shirt.

"You like fighting?" he asked.

I nodded again.

"Like me to teach you?"

"No," I said. "I just like to watch boxing and wrestling sometimes."

I could sense something, feel it, smell it. This was a dangerous man, a man I had to get away from.

"Thanks for helping me," I said, "but I'm all right now. You can get off at your station if you want to."

"Why don't you get off with me?" he asked.

"What?"

"Yeah," he said, "you can come to my apartment and watch television with me."

I knew not to panic, though panic is what I felt. I looked down the car, still crowded as we approached the 180th Street station. Good, I thought, I can make a scene if I have to. My stomach ached. Just don't panic. I remembered that my grandmother thought I was in school and the school principal thought I was home. No one knew where I was. Don't think about it, I told myself. Just don't panic.

"No," I said, "I've got to get home — but thanks again for getting me on the right train."

The doors opened at 180th Street. I stepped out onto the platform, the only child in a crowd of several dozen adults. The man stepped with me.

"Do you know what train to catch from here?" he asked.

"Yeah," I said, "thanks."

He started talking about his boxing career, whom he had fought, how he had been cheated, how he couldn't get good fights anymore, how he had become a sparring partner, and how, to earn "regular" money, he worked as a construction laborer.

I saw my train approach the station. Again he asked, "Sure you don't want to come to my apartment?"

"I can't," I said, and stepped into the subway car. He followed me. Just don't panic.

As the train screeched along, station signs speeding by, his tone changed.

"Why won't you come with me?"

It didn't sound like a question.

I knew the 241st Street station was only a few minutes ahead, but I was trapped. The fighter stood between me and the door. Only a handful of subway riders were in the car.

"C'mon," he argued, his tone harsh. "Let's go watch television in my apartment!"

Although he spoke loudly, angrily, the few people in the car seemed not to hear a word. An older man looked away when I glanced toward him. I was on my own, and I knew it. Just don't panic.

"I can't," I said.

"Don't you like me?"

"Sure."

"Then why not?"

I tried to be steady, but my voice trembled anyway: "I have . . . to go home."

He placed his hand on my shoulder and squeezed. I could feel my legs weaken. My stomach ached. I wanted to cry, to scream. Just don't panic.

"I know about boys like you," he said. "What do you want?"

"Nothing," I told him.

"Then how come you went to Times Square?"

"Only to buy this," I said, and as I lifted my left arm to show him the identification bracelet, I could see through the subway window that the train was pulling into the 241st Street station.

"Let me see that," he said, grabbing my wrist.

The doors opened. Just don't panic. My pulse was racing. Think, think.

"Hey!" I yelled.

The unexpected scream startled him, and before he could react, I wrenched my wrist away, ducked under his arm, and tried to leap through the doors behind him. I lost my balance as I jumped, though, and stumbled to the subway platform on my hands and knees, my eyeglasses falling from my face.

Then I panicked.

My glasses had landed almost at the feet of a man who was sweeping litter with a broom in his left hand and a long-handled dustpan in his right. He was an older man, his hair was white, and he was black.

"Help me," I pleaded, sobbing and shouting. "Help me!" I threw my arms around his legs and tightly clutched my hands together.

The fighter, swearing, stepped off the train and reached for me. "That's my little brother," he said.

"I'm not!" I screamed.

"Outta here!" the old man threatened, raising his dustpan high. "Or I'll split your punk head wide open!"

The fighter cursed.

"Call a cop!" the old man shouted toward the platform steps.

The fighter cursed again, then turned and stepped back onto the train.

"You okay, boy?" the old man asked.

I nodded.

"Sure?"

I nodded again.

"Did he hurt you?"

"No," I said, sniffling as I looked up at the old man. "He didn't get a chance."

I picked my glasses up.

"Thank you," I said.

"You sure you're okay?"

"Yeah," I told him. "I just want to go home now."

He patted me on the shoulder. "Go on, boy," he said.

Twenty minutes later I walked into the kitchen of our apartment, my eyes red and puffy from crying. It was more than an hour before the time I would normally return from school.

"Walter, what's the matter?" my grandmother asked, startled by my appearance and concerned that I was early.

"I don't feel well," I said.

How much confidence we have as we face risks later in our lives, how easily we can separate ourselves from what is familiar to us, is a measure of our maturity. As some psychologists contend, it may also stem to some degree from the first lessons of trust we experience, particularly those wrenching times in our infancy when we're separated from the person who cares for us. More, the risks of our childhood — how we learn to trust ourselves and others — remain risks we face all our lives:

Can I be myself?

Can I say what I feel?

Can I be loved?

We know that children can risk far more than they imagine, as I did after I spotted that trinket in the Times Square store window and declared, "I *have* to have that bracelet." Looking back, I realize that I was like the basketball player found scrambling on his knees outside the stadium after the big game.

"What're you lookin' for?" asked his coach.

"My contact lens," reported the player.

"When did you lose it?"

"During the game."

"I don't get it!" the coach exclaimed. "Why are you lookin' *here?*"

"Everything's turned off inside," the player explained. "There's more light here."

Not only must we search in the right place to gain insight, but we must also recognize what we're looking for. Let's see what we can learn from one of the world's most renowned entertainers, a star who is about to search her past.

The little girl lived with her sister and her grandmother in a tiny, disheveled room in a building at the corner of Yucca and Wilcox, only a block from Los Angeles' famous Hollywood Boulevard. Her parents, who lived apart, were both alcoholic, and Nanny, her grandmother, could be called eccentric. Life often was noisy, confusing, and unpredictable for this little girl. She found, though, that she could draw a shade when the world became too unpleasant — that she could close her eyes and through her imagination escape to a better place, a land of fantasy where she could be whoever, wherever she wanted to be. "I am . . ." she'd think, and she was.

Years later, at twenty-six, she would make her Broadway debut in *Once Upon a Mattress*, followed at the Huntington Hartford Theater in Hollywood by *Fade Out–Fade In* and *Plaza Suite*. She'd perform in *I Do, I Do* and *Same Time Next Year*. Her movies would include *Pete 'n' Tillie, The Front Page, The Four Seasons, Annie*, and, on cable television, *Between Friends*. Her TV show would last eleven seasons and would be one of the most watched variety programs ever. The American Guild of Variety Artists would call her the country's out-standing comedienne five times. She would be the second woman to be named to the TV Academy Hall of Fame, and she'd receive a Peabody award, five Emmy awards, six Golden Globe awards, and ten People's Choice awards as America's favorite all-around female entertainer. A Gallup poll, not surprisingly, would report her to be one of the nation's twenty most admired women. Her autobiography, which she would actually write herself, would be the 1986 best seller *One More Time*. Yes, Carol Burnett would be hailed throughout the world for her talent — but I suspected that her career really began back in the building at Yucca and Wilcox, there in Apartment 102, a small room strewn with yellowed newspapers and wrinkled grocery bags, a home she shared with her younger sister, Chris, and Nanny. Thus, as Carol sat across from me in the Garden Terrace Restaurant in Los Angeles one morning a few days before Christmas 1986, I hoped to find the child, the little girl who had, alone, plumbed the rich resources of her own mind years before.

I thought I knew where to start. "Carol," I asked, "how would you define risk?"

"Off the top of my head?"

"Yes," I said, "right off the top."

"A choice," she replied. "That's it, a choice. And now that I think about it, that's a curious answer."

"Why?"

"I wonder," she said, "whether I perceived the big choices I've faced in my own life as risks when I took them. I don't think I did, because basically I'm a chicken. I don't think it occurred to me that I had a real choice. Look, I could have stayed home instead of flying to New York to audition when I was just starting out, but to me, that would have been far more painful than the anxiety I felt about trying."

The ten o'clock sunlight, shining clearly through the large windows of the Garden Terrace, brightened the corner table where we sat and seemed to lighten Carol's short, neatly cut, light brown hair. She was wearing a simple blue and white checked dress with large white buttons, small gold earrings cut in circles, and two gold bracelets — one, I noticed, engraved with the word *Kalola*, which is Hawaiian for Carol.

I remembered how we had walked together along Fifty-Seventh Street in Manhattan one spring afternoon a few months earlier, and how we had turned a corner and nearly stepped on a drunken man who had propped himself up along the edge of a building, a small brown paper bag tightly clutched in one hand, before passing out. Carol had been startled and had grabbed my arm. Her face had paled and she had said, "When I see someone like this, I think about my father."

"I understand," I had told her.

Now, as she spoke, her blue eyes widening and narrowing in emphasis, a word came to me: warm. Carol Burnett is warm. It's not so much that she's liked; she's *loved*. Carol is a star who enjoys her celebrity, but with no pretension, no denial; she's one of the most generous people I've met. Even on this day, when in less than an hour she would be autographing copies of *One More Time* at Brentano's in the Beverly Wilshire Hotel across town, she had found time in a tight schedule to see a friend — me. I was determined not to waste a minute.

"Carol," I asked, "have you taken a risk that failed?"

"Sure," she said. "Lots of projects that I've liked have flopped. What I've learned, though, is that if I like my own performance, I'm not nearly as bothered as I am when I don't like what I've done. That's when I want to kick myself — when something I've done flops and I don't like my work. If I like what I've done — even if no one else likes it — I can handle the failure much easier."

"Do you get upset when a risk you take doesn't work out?"

"Yes, I do."

"How long do you stay upset?"

"Until something replaces it."

"Carol," I asked, "do you make that happen?"

"I think I do," she said. Then she paused, folding her hands on the table. "I think," she began again, "there are times when you want to pull the covers up, put your thumb in your mouth, and have your mommy hold you. We all feel that way, no matter how old we get. During the past three years I've had no one to depend on — no one except me. I was divorced in 1984 after twenty years. I was really depressed, Walter. I'm fifty-three. I didn't know where my life was going."

"What did you do?"

"Well," she said, "at first either I'd keep my bathrobe on and stay in my hotel room or I'd fly off somewhere, expecting, I guess, to find Shangri-la at my next destination. Of course I found no paradise, either in my room or anywhere else. I had no roots."

"What did you do?"

"I started to write my autobiography in earnest — first a word, then a sentence, then a page."

"What did you find?"

"My own little corner," she said. "The book in a very personal way became my home. Funny, isn't it? Today I feel better about myself. I have greater self-esteem, and in a real sense that stems from being uncomfortable."

"Uncomfortable?"

"Yes, *un*comfortable. I suspect that if I had had a real home during this period of my life, *One More Time* might not have been written."

"Carol," I asked, "was there a moment, or a time, when you felt close to the little girl you used to be?"

She nodded. "Yes," she said, "and it reminds me of the kind of episode you'd expect to see on *The Twilight Zone*. It's the only time in my life anything like this occurred, and it was as real as the sunlight coming into this room this morning."

"What happened?"

"I was writing a scene in which Momma and Nanny were arguing with each other while my younger sister, Chrissie, and I played in the same room. Chrissie was fussing with her toy, a knickknack shelf, that she pretended was a doll, an eerie plywood thing that looked headless when she'd dress it. I was fourteen at the time and was painting with watercolors. I remember that I was trying to make different shades of blue. So there were the two of us playing, while Nanny and Momma had at it. The way we ignored the shouting, you would have thought we were deaf! That was how I was writing the end of this particular story, marveling at how kids put up a wall, how they seem to keep going despite the uproar around them. And then —" She paused.

"Then?"

"— and then it was as if I found myself in the room with Chrissie and the young Carol. The older Carol, me, put her hand on the younger Carol's shoulder while she painted a sky with her blue paint; the shouting was loud in the room behind us. 'You'll get through this,' I told her. 'It will be okay.' Then I seemed to pop back to the present. Three hours had passed! Did it happen? Was it self-hypnosis? Now, the truth is that I have no memory of anyone touching me on the shoulder when I was fourteen. But on the other hand, I think that I always knew that things would work out. Did it really happen? I don't know."

"What would you say to that fourteen-year-old girl if she were sitting across from you today?" I asked.

" 'We're still struggling,' I'd say, 'but we're making it.' "

"Would you tell her not to be afraid?"

She nodded.

"I would," she said, "and I hope she'd tell *me* not to be afraid. When you grow up like I did, in some ways you lose being a child. You're too busy acting like a grownup. I was so serious. I played a lot, imagined a lot, but I also took care of Chrissie — dodged the bullets, so to speak. I was a little adult, trying to blend in with the wallpaper. It's very difficult for a child to stay a child when there's alcoholism and tension, never-ending tension. I didn't have the freedom to express myself, to just be a kid. I was told, 'Shut up!' — and I shut up. I understand now more than ever, as we've discussed before, that to find ourselves, we must find the child. To this very day I have difficulty expressing myself on a one-to-one basis. Sometimes I'll stutter in a conversation with one person. I can be intimate with large groups because from the very first, people in audiences made me feel liked. Unconditionally. No strings. Strangers liked me. I'm still more comfortable with ten thousand than with one."

"You haven't stuttered once in this conversation."

"Thank goodness!"

"Carol," I said, "now I'd like to ask you some difficult questions, because —"

"*Difficult?*" she interrupted, laughing. "These haven't been easy."

I laughed too. "We still have some time."

"Okay," she said, "shoot."

"If I had asked you ten years ago to describe your greatest risk, what would you have told me?"

"Probably I would have said it was making the decision to stop doing my television show. What would I do next? The show had been my life for eleven years; the people I worked with were a second family for me. What would *we* do? We had a schedule. We were comfortable with each other. The network asked us to come back for a twelfth year, but I felt caution. I knew in my heart that we should stop. No matter how much we loved what we were doing, we were too close to feeding off ourselves. Now, in show business, as in any business, you either stop before the product sours or finally someone else will make the decision for you. It was scary. But it was the right decision."

"Today what would you say has been your greatest risk?"

"The one I'm taking right now," she said, "and that's having divorced after twenty years of marriage, pulling up my roots, living out of suitcases. It's disorienting. There have been times over the past three years when I've felt like I was treading in quicksand."

"Do you regret it?"

"No," she said, "I don't. Even with the loneliness, the self-doubt, the uncertainty." She paused. "These feelings still exist in me," she continued, "but Walter, I have a tomorrow. A *tomorrow!*"

"What's most important to you?"

"My daughters," she said, "and my work."

"What are you most afraid of now?"

"That I'll wake up one morning," she said, "and discover that I have no goal. *That* would be frightening."

"Do you feel exhilarated?"

"Encouraged, not exhilarated — but I know deep inside me that I'll feel exhilarated again, that there will be one more hurrah, maybe even —" she laughed. "— *two.*"

"Are you preparing yourself?"

"I sure am."

"How?"

"By changing, growing. I needed to change. Alone, slowly, day by day, I stopped wallowing. Looking inside myself, 'finding the child' as I've heard you call it, I began to see what I was gaining, not just what I was losing. I understand now that what's most important is how I've grown — and what I've gained from the experience."

"What's that?"

When she spoke, her words were even, firm.

"I understand," she said, "that *only I can change my life*. No one can do it for me. Do you know what else has helped me? The thought that if I handle myself well, I'll be showing my daughters, by example, that when it's their turn, they too can get through what's basically a midlife crisis. No one escapes real life. If we live long enough, we live it all — and I think that some of the worst pain we experience as adults is caused by the baggage we've picked up along the way. Some things we've learned — or have been taught! — weaken our resolve to take risks."

"Remember the child?"

"Yes!" she said. "On the one hand, it's important for me to remember the Carol who had to blend into that apartment at Yucca and Wilcox, but on the other, it's even more important for me as an adult to remember the Carol who was willing — no, *eager* — to take a risk. How could I have assessed the risk I was taking by flying off to New York to audition for a role? Kids hear all the time, 'You can't do this, you can't do that,' but they don't count the odds. Look, nothing's changed. We have to remember that when we don't allow ourselves to be blinded by the odds, we're more able to face the everyday risks we encounter. And we have to deal with the truth about being embarrassed."

"Which is?"

"That only *we* can embarrass ourselves. The most I've ever been humiliated is when I've pussyfooted, when I've been unprepared, when I haven't plunged right in. Look at it this way: I put my toe in the water, then my leg — gee, it's chilly! —

then I'm in up to my waist, and as I look up, the boat's sailed! We must dive in.

"My daughter Erin, for example, complained to me one day: 'Oh, Mom, I had a terrible audition at school.'

"I asked her, 'Did you know what you were going to do before you stepped on-stage?' "

" 'No,' she told me, 'I didn't.'

"I asked, 'When you held out your arms to sing, how far did you stretch them out? This far?' " — Carol gently, almost shyly, lifted her arms off the table. " 'Or *this* far?' " Carol threw her arms wide with enthusiasm, nearly toppling a pitcher of coffee.

"Hold it!" I said. "I'm not in this show."

"That's it!" she said, laughing. "If you're going to attempt something new, don't try it, *do* it. Go full out. If you're going to make a mistake, make a big one. Good entertainers do that all the time. They barrel ahead. It's worse to be wishy-washy than to be wrong.

"Once I had the opportunity to be a guest on *The Dinah Shore Show,* and I fibbed to get on. They asked me, 'Can you ice-skate?' 'Of course,' I lied. I'd never been on ice skates in my life. I had, however, been on roller skates. It was a week until rehearsal. Quickly I found an ice palace, rented skates, and hung on for dear life. Fortunately, when I was a child I was quite a roller skater. I visualized the blades as wheels. I practiced like the devil, and rehearsal day arrived — too quickly, I thought.

"I did okay. No prizes, mind you — okay. 'Oh,' I was told, 'you've skated before.'

" 'Uh huh,' " I said.

"Now the thing is that the same person who took that risk, me, actually lived a Charlie Brown life until only recently. I would do things, say yes, because I didn't want anyone to be upset with me. Can you imagine? 'Good old Carol.' It took me all these years to understand that saying no doesn't mean I'm nasty, selfish, or unlikable in any way. Saying no when you really want to say no is honest. The problem, of course, is finding and coming to terms with the child inside me, the girl who tried to blend into the wallpaper at Yucca and Wilcox. I've come a long way now that I can say I understand that maybe everyone can't love us — and that's fine too."

"Are these going to be better years?"

"Yes," she said, "I think they will be. Once you face your problems honestly, once you come out the other side, the years are better. You know why?"

"Why?"

"Because you know you can survive. And that is a good thing to know."

"Carol," I asked, "do you like yourself more today?"

"I sure do."

"Even one-on-one?"

"I'm working on it."

I report Carol's story because there's a lesson within a lesson in her remarkable life. It reminds me of the ancient tale of the little eagle that refused to look at itself.

Quite by accident, as the fable is told, a farmer found an eagle's egg on a hill, carried it to the chicken coop near his barn, and plopped it alongside some eggs in the nest of a hen. Thus the eagle hatched among a brood of chicks.

As the eagle grew it did what chickens do, since it was convinced that it was a chicken. It clucked. It flapped its wings to fly a few feet in the air. Like the other chickens, it searched for no more exotic food than the seeds and insects it found by scratching the earth.

One day it looked up into the sky and saw the most dazzling creature it had ever seen.

"What is that?" it asked, startled by the sheer majesty of the form soaring gracefully in wide circles in and out of the high clouds.

"That," a rooster said in a hushed, reverent tone, "is an eagle, the greatest of all birds."

"Wow, I'd like to do that!"

"Forget it," the rooster advised. "We're different."

So the little eagle forgot — and when it died a year later, it died believing it was a chicken.

Do you recognize the little eagle? Sometimes that's us, isn't it?

Fortunately, one of the many things that we can learn from Carol Burnett is that we have the capacity, if we tap into it, to soar from our nests. We can examine our own experiences — we too can find the child within ourselves — and we can grow. When it seems safer to cluck, remember: *We were made to soar.*

You've taken a step in that direction, made an act of trust, by reading this book. Stay with me. Take another step, one that begins by recognizing a basic law of learning: *Organisms repeat responses that have brought satisfaction in the past; often these responses persist even when they no longer bring satisfaction.*

It's true of a simple protozoan, and it's true of a complex human being. Almost every freshman psychology student learns how Nobel laureate Ivan Pavlov's dogs salivated at the sound of a bell, even when they were no longer rewarded with food.

How about us?

It would be rare for anyone not to have acted childlike at least once while facing some adult risk — not to have repeated behavior, however inappropriate, learned in his or her earliest years. For example, I know I've pretended at times that something I've really wanted, but was afraid to take a risk for, was not important to me. I'll bet you have too. When we deny what we really desire, we most resemble a small child shouting, "I don't want that toy anyway!"

Inevitably, when we try to escape risk, when we limit our opportunities to grow, to *soar*, we feel more helpless, more dependent, more vulnerable — in other words, more childlike. Confidence, in the end, comes from doing. And to know what we're doing when we consider the crucial risks of our lives — to muster our courage — we need to understand not only what but how we've learned. After all, we are what we think. The world in which we live is shaped by how we see it. To one person, what lies ahead is scorched earth; to another, a field to be plowed. So it is with risk. One of us learns to see danger; another, opportunity.

And we can learn to see more clearly. To sharpen our vision, we must understand how deeply the old, familiar ways are ingrained in our personalities. Early on, we're taught to avoid certain risks: Don't touch this! Don't swallow that! Other risks are encouraged: Walk, walk! Oh, you fell! You're okay. You can do it. Keep trying!

When we're young, independence rarely brings rewards. Rebellious responses often inspire guilt, or punishment. Also, much of what we remember from childhood glows with a halo of virtue: Our elders were bigger, stronger, wiser; they *loved* us. Who are we to question their teachings?

Some of our most profound lessons are taught with subtlety, almost as if they are not taught but absorbed. Consider an extreme:

We're riding down the street in the family car, Daddy at the wheel.

"Bang! Bang! Bang!" we shout, aiming our imaginary pistols at streetlights, road signs, trees, pretending all to be villains we're about to vanquish.

"Hold on," says Daddy, laughing. "Hold your fire for a nigger!"

A child learns to trust.

What pleases Daddy? Although a racist may argue that his bias is rooted in some evidence, some graphic experience he can relate, and is thus reasoned and mature, the hard truth is that his hatred bursts from his darkest corners, his insecurity, and it is self-consuming and childlike.

The human mind is like a doorway. When we have no opinion, the opening is as wide as can be. Give us some information, and the door closes slightly. A little more, perhaps spiced with a smile from Daddy, and the door closes further. Ask us a question about what we've learned — thereby encouraging us to commit ourselves to a position — and the door is only slightly ajar, if open at all.

Some of our strongest views, of course, are healthy and necessary. No one should be able to persuade us to stick our thumb into a live socket, unwillingly surrender our freedom, drive down the wrong side of the road. On the other hand, you've probably known a child who breaks no rules because he's not so sure his folks really love him and he doesn't want to test the premise. I've known adults who try to please parents who are long dead, parents who were incapable of accepting or understanding their children. I suspect that if I had not faced the truth about my own father, a violent alcoholic, and if I had not resolved the real conflict between us when I was a young adult, I too would be glancing over my shoulder. Thus, I'm sure that the challenge for each of us, when reflecting on our childhood, is to avoid being like Mark Twain's cat, which, once burned, would sit on neither a hot stove nor a cold one.

Growing up requires us to face risks, to stretch, to try activities that are at the limit of or just beyond our demonstrated abilities. At each step we risk failure. We need support, the encouragement of others. I can remember a time in my own childhood when I reached for esteem — and learned some lessons.

I had tried several times to get into the poolroom a couple of blocks from the tenement in which I was raised.

"Can I just watch?"

"No," I was told, "you're too young."

It was 1956, and I had been playing pool seriously for nearly three years, mainly at the Mount Vernon Boys Club, but also wherever else I could find a table. The poolroom near my home, though, was where I desperately wanted to play. Some of the best black players from lower Westchester County and the Bronx shot pool there. I wanted to watch them — and I wanted to play against them. It's not that I was a good player; I was a good *twelve-year-old* player. I was sure I could win on a big "spot," which meant that if I played an adult who had some skill, I could expect him to spot me some balls — give me a handicap — maybe five or six in a game of twenty-five, or ten to twelve in a game of fifty.

Unexpectedly, I was given my chance one Saturday afternoon when several of us sat waiting — impatiently waiting — for a turn at the table in the Boys Club. The larger boys were playing — interminably, it seemed.

"You guys ever going to finish?" I asked.

They laughed.

I shrugged.

"Man, hurry up!" a boy named Jimmy shouted. He was black, about my age and size, and he lived in a public housing project only a couple of blocks from my home.

"You talking to *me*?" the largest boy asked, the tone of his question threatening, bullying.

"Jimmy," I said, "be cool."

"I don't sweat him," Jimmy told me.

"I know," I said, "but there's no sense in us getting kicked out."

"Listen to your man," the larger boy warned, referring to me. Had that been all he said, the quarrel probably would have ended there. However, he added, "*punk!*"

It was a brief fight. The two larger boys overpowered us quickly, but fortunately for Jimmy and me, the fracas was stopped by counselors before we were hurt.

As we walked home, Jimmy and I boldly described to each other how well we had done against the bigger guys, the memory considerably larger than the truth. When we neared the public project in which Jimmy lived with his father, he suggested, "Let's go to the poolroom on Third Street."

"You have to be sixteen," I said.

"If you can keep your mouth shut," he told me, "I can get us in."

"How?" I asked.

"My old man," he said.

"What's that mean?"

"My old man plays every day. If I'm with him, they say nothing. Come on."

"What about *me?*" I asked, tapping my face.

He laughed. "It's all right," he assured me, "if you're with my old man."

"Okay," I said, "let's go."

Jimmy's father was not enthusiastic. "No," he said.

Jimmy pleaded, telling his father how we had fought side by side at the Boys Club. He somewhat exaggerated our success — I think he said we won! — and finally, reluctantly, his father agreed to take us.

When I played Jimmy's father that afternoon in a game of twenty-five, he beat me by more than a dozen balls.

"You're okay," he told me, though. "If you practice some, you'll be good."

For several days thereafter, whenever I could be sure that Jimmy's father would be playing pool, I walked in. One afternoon, though, I opened the door, and Jimmy's father wasn't there! My pulse quickened. I'm going to be thrown out, I worried. A second passed, then another. An old man by the cash register absently nodded to me. I nodded back. Then I understood; I belonged.

From that moment, whenever I arrived home from school, I'd hurry to complete a daily newspaper route I had in the Bronx, then I'd return quickly to Mount Vernon to the poolroom. Nights, weekends, days off, whole weeks, then months I practiced — a quarter a rack, nearly every day. The few dollars I earned each week were devoted to a single end: pool.

Several players knew my father, who did not play pool, who *hated* poolrooms, whose drinking and violent temper stood out even in our neighborhood. It was no surprise, then, that no one, not even the folks he drank with, chose to tell him that his son was hanging out in a poolroom a couple of blocks away. He was unpredictable, volatile, a person to be approached with caution. One minute he was a gentle soul; the next, dangerous.

"Where are you going?" my mother would ask.

"Out," I'd reply, "with my friends — I'll be home early."

"Stay out of trouble," she'd warn me. Understanding what I'd face if my father found out, I did.

Of the memories of my childhood, none are more vivid than the poolroom smell of cigarettes, usually Kools and Pall Malls, and beer, usually Rheingold or Schaefer's, the satiny feel of green felt, the dusty blue chalk, and the sounds — Chuck Berry's "Roll Over Beethoven," Fats Domino's "My Blue Heaven" and "Blueberry Hill," Ray Charles's "Hallelujah I Love Her

So," Little Richard's "Long Tall Sally," "Rip It Up," and "Lu-cille," all heard behind the crack of the balls, the laughter, and sometimes the silence — silence when something unusual was about to happen: an especially difficult shot, a big money shot, or occasionally an argument. Players roared when someone retold a joke of Moms Mabley's or Slappy White's, but it was an album called *Laff of the Party* by Redd Foxx that brought players to tears, laughing as they held their sides.

Of hundreds of players, few knew my name. They called me "you" or "boy" or "kid," until I earned a new nickname, a story that began one afternoon when I played Jimmy's father a game of twenty-five.

"I'll spot you ten balls," he offered, "and we'll play for game," which meant that the loser paid for the use of the table.

"You sure you want to spot me *ten* balls?" I asked.

"Sure," he said, "why?"

I boasted, "I can beat Willie Mosconi" — who was known as one of the greatest players in the world — "with a ten-spot."

He laughed. "Boy, you'd have to beat me to play him. Maybe I better spot you five, since you're so good."

"I'll take the ten," I said, smiling widely, "so I can win this game quick."

He laughed louder.

Outside, such talk might have earned me a quick, stinging response, but inside, chatter was part of the game. It was the language, the bravura, the bluster, the swagger of the time and place — and I was a player.

"Rack them, kid," he told me.

Jimmy's father promptly ran nine balls, barely missing the tenth; it hovered, hesitated, but didn't fall into a corner pocket. Because of the ten-spot, I was one ball ahead before I raised my cue.

I ran five balls, a sixth on the break, then four more. The score was twenty to nine, my favor.

Jimmy's father ran thirteen balls. The score was twenty-two to twenty, his favor.

The poolroom grew quiet. Several players watched our table. Jimmy's father rarely lost. We were playing a good game — and I could win, because he had left me in a good position on a table with more than twice as many balls as I'd need.

Twenty-one.

Twenty-two; tied.

Twenty-three; my favor.

Twenty-four.

I had a choice. I could take a bank shot, which is to hit a ball off the cushion into the side pocket, or take what looked like the riskier shot, sending the cue ball down the table into a combination, so the first ball would strike a second into the corner pocket. I circled the table to study the balls. The combination, I realized, looked more difficult than it really was. If the cue ball struck the first ball flush and center, the second ball would almost leap into the pocket. The bank shot was even easier, but less spectacular; it was the "money" shot, the safe shot to take.

With all eyes on me, I signaled the combination. Some bets were made. I heard Jimmy's father. He bet against me!

I looked up at him.

He smiled.

Why would Jimmy's father bet that I'd miss? He knew that the combination wasn't as tough as it looked, that I was . . . well, showboating. What, I wondered, did he see? I checked the shot again. He raised his bet.

I leaned over the table, ready to shoot. I hesitated, again studying the distance between the cue ball and the first ball to hit. This is easy, I told myself. But what is it that he sees? What am I missing? The room was silent. I drew the cue back, the pulse pounding in my temple.

I missed. In fact, I scratched, sending the cue ball straight into the corner pocket.

I was speechless.

Mercifully, the sounds of the poolroom resumed, because no one doubted what would happen next. Jimmy's father ran three balls. The game was over; I was a loser.

Embarrassed, I left.

How did he know?

I had to find out. The following afternoon I approached Jimmy's father.

"You knew all along I should have taken the bank shot, didn't you?"

"No," he said, shaking his head, "that wasn't it. I would have bet you'd miss the bank too."

"Why," I asked, "when that was a sure shot?"

"Boy," he told me, "I wasn't betting against the shot —"

"I don't understand," I interrupted.

"— I was betting against *you*."

"I still don't understand," I said, perplexed.

"You let me talk you out of it," he explained, his voice patient. "You heard me bet and you got worried that I knew something, didn't you?"

I nodded.

"Well, that was nothing but me talking you out of an easy shot. I knew that if you thought hard enough about the bet, you'd probably miss."

"What if I had made the shot?"

"You didn't."

I nodded again. "You think I'll ever beat you?" I asked.

He paused. "You might," he said, then laughed. "When you're an old man."

I started to walk away.

He stopped me. "Heart," he told me, hitting his chest. "That counts more than skill most of the time. Boy, all these guys can shoot pool, but if the bet's right, most of them will fold — now don't feel bad! — just like you did. The bet that cracks one might be twenty bucks, another a hundred, or maybe a thousand. *Something*. Sure, sometimes they make their shot, but over time they'll miss more than they'll make. And you know why they'll miss?"

"Why?"

"Because they'll think about the stakes, not the shot. 'How big's the bet?' That's when they start losing heart, when they start asking themselves, 'Can I make this shot?' "

"That's when *you* bet?"

"Right," he said. "You want to win?"

I nodded.

"Then remember that the size of a bet can mess you up only if you let it."

"Don't pay attention to it?"

"No," he said, "you don't want to ignore it. You'd only be kidding yourself anyway. You *know* the bet's there. But instead of concentrating on the stakes, what you need to do is to try to remember how you've made the same shot before. Then, before you even pick up your cue, get the shot going in your mind. Imagine the cue ball rolling down the table, hitting the next ball just right — and there, it drops in the pocket."

"All right!" I exclaimed. "Want to play some pool?"

He laughed loudly.

"Not today," he said.

He was in the poolroom several weeks later, however, when I played the game of my life. It was a Saturday afternoon, and I was playing fifty with an older man when I started a run with my thirty-second ball.

Thirty-three.

Thirty-four.

Thirty-nine.

Forty.

Forty-nine.

My last ball was a bank shot in the side.

Fifty.

I had run nineteen balls, the most ever for me.

"Keep going!" someone shouted.

I continued shooting.

At twenty-five, a combination into the side pocket, Jimmy's father bet — that I'd make it.

I did.

At thirty I had only one shot, a difficult shot for me, a long table shot off the cushion. There were several bets. I noticed Jimmy's father was quiet. He made no bet, but he did smile.

I leaned over the table to study the angle. I can do this, I thought. I pictured it in my mind. More bets. My pulse raced. *Think about the shot.* I drew back the cue.

I made the shot — and the next. Then I missed.

A run of thirty-one! Although I would not approach thirty-one again, the feat earned me a nickname.

"Boy," someone called me after the game.

"That's no boy," Jimmy's father told him, "that's 'Run.'"

For nearly a month I was greeted with "Hey, Run, want to shoot a game?"

One morning a new player, misunderstanding the nickname, called me "Runt."

"*Run*," I corrected — and several players chuckled.

Then one Saturday afternoon, as I was stretched across one of the tables taking a shot, I heard my real name shouted — "Walter!" — and my skin tingled. Standing in the open door-way was my father, his face red, the veins of his neck working, his hands balled into fists. No one moved.

"Get home *now!*" he bellowed.

I reached into my pocket, nervously grabbed two quarters to pay for the game, and dropped both on the table felt.

"Move!" he shouted.

I walked briskly to the door. I tried to slide past him, but he cuffed me on the back of the head, a slap that sent me sprawling to the pavement outside.

"If I ever find my son in here again," he threatened, his words slow, his voice low and deep through clenched teeth, "I will close this place."

Still no one moved.

"*Ever!*" he added.

He beat me on the way home, in the apartment that afternoon, and again that night. Crying did not help.

"You want to cry?" my father asked menacingly. "Here, I'll give you something to cry about!"

Smack.

"You will *never* go in there again!" he shouted.

I didn't. Nor did I ever play pool seriously again.

Let me ask, what is it that you do not now have, need, but are afraid to reach for? This is the essence of every risk, isn't it? From our first breath, we desire *more*.

Whatever we seek — love, power, self-esteem — what stands in our way?

Losses.

When we face a risk, isn't our chief concern what we may lose? Yet ironically, more often than not we fail to identify clearly what those losses might be. Sometimes all we have is a vague, queasy feeling that we're going to lose *something*. By itself, that shadowy suspicion has stopped me in my tracks more than once. When I can't identify my losses, my anxiety blossoms, as it did when Jimmy's father bet against me. I've found that at the very moment when the pressure to take a risk is greatest, I have the strongest impulse to retreat.

Fortunately, I've learned that to take risks intelligently, I must appreciate three losses contained in every worthwhile risk:

The positive loss.

The practical loss.

The potential loss.

The first of these, the *positive loss*, is a loss of innocence, a loss of comfort. Once we acknowledge that what we have isn't enough, we cannot kid ourselves that we're satisfied. The positive loss is an honest loss, a mature loss, a loss of ignorance. We must recognize, though, that it causes us to choose: We must either try to achieve what we desire or be frustrated. Pretending we're happy when we're not is an unwillingness to take a positive loss; we *know* we want more.

Taking a positive loss is a far more active step than it may seem at first glance. It's what I did when I realized I wouldn't be satisfied until I won at pool and proved myself against adults. And it's what Carol Burnett meant when she said, "I don't think it occurred to me that I had a real choice. Look, I could have stayed home when I was just starting out, but to me, that would have been far more painful than the anxiety I felt about trying."

The second loss contained in every worthwhile risk, the *practical loss*, is what we give up to go ahead. Sometimes it's obvious. To take a new job, for example, we must give up the old one. To live away at college, we must leave home. At other times a practical loss can be hidden, as in the lame excuse "I could if I tried." False security is the practical loss here. At risk is self-esteem: "If I don't try, I can't fail."

When I challenged adult pool players, I lost the easy security of winning against children of my age. Carol Burnett could have failed too: "Lots of projects that I've liked have flopped." Although a positive loss rivets our attention by forcing us to choose, we find the heartbeat, the epicenter, of our anxiety in our *practical* losses. Most of us, like soldiers at war, will struggle far more strenuously to hold onto what we have than to gain something new. It's not easy to let go.

The third loss, the *potential loss*, is the tangible thing that we lose only if the risk does not work out — and it's usually the easiest to identify and the most discussed. Ask, what if I don't succeed? In a marriage, like Carol's, the *positive* loss is the recognition of dissatisfaction, which can lead to the *practical* loss of a spouse. The *potential* loss for Carol and for other married people is, of course, the security of the familiar: What if no one ever loves me? Will I be alone? Will I feel lonely?

My potential losses became my actual losses when my father found me in the poolroom. Let's see now what losses we can find in the story of an authentic hero, one of America's more colorful leaders.

It was an early autumn afternoon in 1987 and I was on an upper floor at the Pentagon. Two naval officers in their twenties, their uniforms neat and their posture erect, strode purposefully to a white door. Then the pair hesitated, seeming to weigh the gravity of the act of opening the door — the entrance to the inner office of the United States secretary of the navy.

The man inside was forty-one, a graduate of both Annapolis and Georgetown University Law School, the best-selling author of *Fields of Fire*, *A Sense of Honor*, and *A Country Such as This*, and a former Marine rifle company commander who had distinguished himself in combat in a place called An Hoa Basin in Vietnam. There his unit suffered fifty-six casualties in two months, and his men, *enlisted* men, asked that their commander be recognized for personal bravery and leadership under fire.

His superiors agreed, and James Webb received the Navy Cross, the country's second highest honor, as well as a Silver Star, two Bronze Stars, and two Purple Hearts. His combat boots were the models for those on the Vietnam memorial statue in Washington, D.C.

It was clear that the navy secretary was a legitimate hero to the young officers outside his door. When the door swung open and they saluted in unison, they meant it, *sir!*

Later, as I sat across from Jim Webb in his office, I remembered how he had once described to me the way in which generations of his family had had to struggle to get by in hard times on hard land, with few dollars but great pride. He and his ancestors, he told me, had fought in seven American wars. Yet this man, whom I had known for five years, did not look like a warrior. He looked more like a teacher, a minister — or a president. His blond hair was thick and full, his blue eyes wide and clear — he looked like the young John Kennedy, I thought, dynamic, smart, and kind. I recalled how quickly he had agreed to rearrange his tight schedule a couple of years earlier, when he was assistant secretary of defense, to present an award on behalf of the New York Vietnam Veterans Leadership Program to Elmo Zumwalt III, a Vietnam veteran facing death from cancer.

It would have been easy, because Jim was a Vietnam War hero, to focus my questions on the risks he faced when he led Marines in combat. I knew, though, that as challenging as his war experience had been, the true test for my friend came later, on the afternoon a doctor told him his military career was over. I hoped he'd share this story with me, a story about losses.

But first I asked, "How did you learn to be so independent?"

He laughed, leaned back in his chair, and lighted a pipe. "I had to learn early to live in an environment of change," he began. "I went to a new school in the fifth grade, the sixth grade, the seventh grade, three different schools in the eighth and ninth grades, two in the tenth. By the time I hit that second school in the tenth grade, if someone said my name wrong, I'd try to punch his lights out. This caused my uncle, who had been a fighter, to suggest that I start to box. In the ring I learned to survive, to rely on myself. I discovered that I had to accept blame when things went wrong — and things *did* go wrong. Also, I learned earlier than most adolescents not to depend on peer acceptance; even the sport I chose, boxing, was solitary.

"In my schoolwork I was unpredictable. If I liked a subject or a particular teacher, I did well. Otherwise, I did only enough to get by. I could have gone in several directions — and not all were wise. About a year ago I was reminded of this, when a friend with whom I had graduated from high school, a fellow I had not seen for a quarter of a century, stopped by to say hello.

" 'Jim,' he told me, 'I always knew that something was going to happen to you, but I never knew whether it would be good or bad.' I was sure he was right. I could have ended up in jail as well as anywhere else."

"What made the difference?"

"The military — the same thing that made the difference for you. It gave me focus. I became the first person in my family to go straight to college when I finished high school. My dad was the first to finish high school — and he attended night school on and off for twenty-six years to receive a college degree. I remember the day he received it. I was a senior in high school. He held his diploma up to my face and said, 'You can get anything you want in this country. And don't you ever forget it.'

"These were the lessons of my childhood. My ancestors might have been called rednecks, but they were the ones, these mountain people, who settled the border states. They had few material goods, but they did have precious values. And what values they are! My grandmother, for example, had this tough Scotch-Irish quiescence. I remember when my father, who had just returned from Alaska, was suddenly ordered to the Berlin airlift. I was a small boy, and I was torn up about losing him, not seeing him again. He said he'd be back in six months. I didn't know what six months meant! What little kid would? My grandmother, though, took me out to the backyard garden.

" 'See the corn we've just planted?' she asked.

"I nodded.

" 'Every day,' she continued, 'you and I are going to come out here and check this corn. It's going to have stalks. Then it's going to have shoots off the stalks. Then it's going to have ears. You understand?'

" 'Yes,' I said.

" 'Then,' she explained, 'it's going to have tassels. When the tassels go brown, we're going to pick the corn. Then we are going to eat the corn, and *then* —'

" 'Then?' I asked.

" '— and *then* your father will come home.'

"Of course, we did just that, and the rest occurred as you'd expect — with my father coming home. Now that's teaching a child to cope, to understand in a real way. It also says a lot about beauty in adversity, character, my grandmother's character, and as I see it, honor."

"How would you define honor?" I asked.

"Honor begins with accepting that what we do, large or small, matters. When I was first appointed here, a *Newsweek* reporter who interviewed me happened to mention how important he thought this job was, and I remember I agreed, but I also told him that when I die, God's not going to ask me if I had been secretary of the navy.

"In fact, a few weeks ago, after I spoke to the assembled midshipmen at the Naval Academy, one raised a question about honor in light of the Iran-contra controversy.

" 'Sir,' he asked me, 'what do you do when you receive orders that you do not believe you can execute?'

" 'Every person in this room,' I told him, 'is going to have to define and weigh the value of his or her own integrity. You cannot violate the principles for which you stand. Honor has no shortcuts; it's wrong to lie, to cheat, to steal.' "

"How do you apply that, Jim, in this office?"

"I'm willing to resign," he said, his voice firm, "and that means now, in the next hour, tomorrow, at any time. I decided years ago, in Vietnam, that the only recommendations my superiors are ever going to receive from me are those that I'm convinced are in the best interests of our nation, and that means within both the letter *and* the spirit of the law. Duty requires me to tell my boss when I think he's wrong — and any appointed official who's not willing to leave his office over high principle is in the job for the wrong reason."

"How do you absorb losses?"

"First, I've come to accept that there are some losses that I cannot redeem. In my last year at Annapolis, for example, I was defeated in my final boxing match for the championship. That may seem like a small thing, but it troubled me for a long time because I knew that I had lost my *last* match and I knew that I'd not get a second chance. Vietnam was another difficult loss, and it had a profound effect on me, as have the loss of friends and the loss of my first marriage. I now understand, though, that to go forward, to grow, we must give up *something*, often something we value. I've found that I can't just absorb a loss and move on. I have to understand it, grapple with it, squeeze some value out of it, learn from it. I've known people who basically ignore their losses. That doesn't work for

me. I'm a confronter. I need to understand what I have lost —
or might lose. When I face a loss, the effort strengthens my
resolve; only when I know what I might lose can I proceed
with confidence."

"Have you faced risks in which you've known only what you
might lose, not what you might gain?"

"Yes," he replied, "and that's the toughest of all."

"Like leaving the Marine Corps?"

"Yes," he said, "and that was the first time I had to take a
really big loss for an unknown risk. That was a major moment
in my life, after I was wounded the second time in Vietnam.
I had been hit all over from shrapnel and after some hospi-
talization, I was returned to my unit. I developed an infection
that the doctors called septic knee. Desperately, I wanted to
stay in the Marine Corps. This, after all, was my life; I knew
no other. My dad had been a career serviceman, and I had no
other goal but to serve. I returned to the States, and for more
than a year I underwent the same kind of therapy that the Jets
quarterback Joe Namath had gone through.

"One afternoon after therapy, the doctor sat down next to
me. 'I'm really impressed with what you're trying to do,' he
said, 'but you can't succeed.'

" 'I can try,' I argued. 'I *will* succeed.'

" 'Not this time,' he told me. 'If you continue this therapy,
within three years your joint will be fused. This is not a sports
injury. You've been badly wounded in combat, and your knee
cannot, under any circumstances, be repaired to the level you'll
need as a Marine.'

" 'What are you telling me?' I asked him.

" 'You're young,' he said. 'You have a lot of life left. Get out
of the service while you can still walk. Frankly, if you keep up
this strenuous exercise, you're going to be crippled. This is not
a challenge you can overcome through your effort and will.

It's not a question of courage. You *can't* win. It's over. Look, I can put you on limited duty, operate again in six months — but the results will be the same.'

" 'No chance?' I asked.

" 'None,' he told me.

"I *can't* win, I realized for the first time. If I won't be an infantry officer one hundred percent, it *is* over. What, I wondered, am I going to do now?

"Ironically, I had been sent to the secretary of the navy's office for duty while I was trying to resolve my medical difficulties. I loved the Marine Corps, and I had just been promoted to captain, a year early. The Marine aide at the time, a colonel, recognized what I was experiencing, and he encouraged me: 'You know what you can't do. Now what do you want to do?'

"I knew the answer, but I didn't know what I could do with it. The answer was to serve our country. That's what I wanted to do. It's all I ever wanted to do. But how?

" 'I have a friend with the Environmental Protection Agency,' he volunteered. 'Maybe he can help you.'

"Now that sounded interesting. The *environment*. I could do a lot of good. I tested for a spot, then worked four days at the EPA. On the fifth day I walked into the supervisor's office:

" 'I'd like to leave,' I said.

"He was incredulous.

" 'You've done more in four days,' he told me, 'than the guy next to you has done in a month.'

"I understood the risk I was taking — this was a safe job, and with a newborn child at home, I'd be losing a lot of security. Nonetheless, I knew it was wrong for me.

" 'I don't want to do this,' I said.

" 'What *do* you want to do?'

" 'I think I'd like to go to law school, but it's too late for me to apply.'

" 'Maybe,' he suggested, 'I can help you.'

"He introduced me to a former Marine drill instructor who had become a successful lawyer. This man interviewed me, then helped my effort to be considered by the admissions process at three different law schools."

"Jim," I asked, "what would you tell the two young officers who were in here earlier about facing losses?"

He sat silent for a few seconds, then nodded.

"I'd give them precisely the same advice I'd give my son," he said. "Before all else, each of us must take a fundamental risk — to be true to ourselves. The Naval Academy taught me that I could not run away from my problems, which is what I did when I did poorly in high school, when I fought at the drop of a hat. I was not confronting my problems; I was avoiding them. There are going to be losses. From them, we grow."

Carol Burnett made a comment earlier that, I think, perfectly describes the hard core of successful risk-taking: "Only I can change my life," she said. "No one can do it for me." Jim Webb too has lived that conviction, and his final advice is essential for all of us: "Before all else, each of us must take a fundamental risk — to be true to ourselves."

It would be foolish to suggest that I could discuss enough in this section (or in this book) to examine the depth and breadth of childhood experience thoroughly. Risk-taking, as I wrote earlier, is too important a process to be trivialized, to play "let's pretend." What I've sought to do here is to encourage you to reflect, as have the people I've interviewed — to search your experience candidly and aggressively for hidden obstacles that can hold you back.

Only I can change my life.

We've seen that to change our lives, to take a risk prudently, we have to do more than analyze risk–reward ratios.

"Kids hear all the time 'You can't do this, you can't do that,' " Carol said, "but they don't count the odds. Look, nothing's changed. . . . When we don't allow ourselves to be blinded by the odds, we're more able to face the everyday risks we encounter."

Only I can change my life.

"Instead of concentrating on the stakes," Jimmy's father wisely advised, "you need to try to remember how you've made the same shot before."

"There are going to be losses," Jim Webb said. "From them, we grow."

Let me share with you now what I perceived as a child to be my greatest risk.

When I was thirteen years old, I made a deal with God.

We came to this understanding early one Sunday in 1957 as I was seated, reluctantly seated, in a rear pew of Immanuel Evangelical Lutheran Church. Though I seem to remember hearing "Rock of Ages" during the service, I'm sure we didn't sing "Amazing Grace." I know if we had sung my favorite hymn, there might be no story to tell, because "Amazing Grace" always humbled me, its haunting notes inexplicably raising goose bumps on my flesh. No, I felt anything but humble that morning.

The sermon seemed to lie like an early morning mist over a lake, the pastor's voice a gentle hum within the heavy silence in the room. As the service continued, the mist ever thickening, heads nodded. My eyes started to droop.

Involuntarily, I chuckled.

The father of a schoolmate, two rows ahead, turned and gave me a stern look. I averted my eyes.

I could feel the warmth of the heavyset woman who sat next to me, her bulk squeezing me tightly into the corner of the pew. Her great body was encased in a dress that suddenly looked to me like a yellow tent.

I smiled.

She frowned.

I stopped smiling.

I sat quietly for what seemed to me an eternity, a peace that in truth probably lasted no more than twenty seconds. Was my leg falling asleep? I moved my toes. No, no pain there. My mind wandered again and I found myself studying some of the parishioners, wondering silently, why do you come here? I saw more heads nod.

Why am I here?

To become a Lutheran, I reminded myself, like most of the other boys and girls in my class at Immanuel Lutheran School. In two Sundays, after I passed an oral exam scheduled in a few days, I would be confirmed.

My classmates and I had dutifully, if not enthusiastically, studied our catechisms. We had memorized endless questions and answers. I worried, though, because the questions were not *my* questions, and I had no answers. After all the instruction, both in school and in church, after all the hours of listening, reading, and listening again, I was troubled. Worse, at thirteen, I was unable to articulate clearly how deeply I was troubled.

Why, I wanted to know, don't Catholics go to heaven? Or Jews? Or Baptists? When I raised the question with my teacher, I was assured that I had been shown the clear path to redemption, and I was even encouraged to spread the word. That wasn't the answer I had hoped for. I needed more. Some of my friends were Catholic, others Jewish. Many were Baptist, black Baptist. My neighborhood, as you might suspect, was a tossed salad of colors and languages, and the children of all of these families, like children elsewhere, played together.

Moreover, my mother, my older brother, and my sister had been raised Protestant but not Lutheran — and the closest my father came to any church was weddings and funerals. What about *them?* This was unsettling. Were my family and many of my friends damned? Why? Is God unfair? *I don't understand.*

Like apples slowly bobbing in a pail of water, more heads nodded among the congregation. Why, I asked myself, am I here? Do I believe?

The question startled me. *Do I believe?* I was sure I was crossing a line, a very dangerous line. We had been warned about just such a moment — we had been warned how clever, how terribly tempting Satan could be, how he could raise doubts. I understood I was risking my very soul. Like a moth, I circled the flame. I tried thinking about something else. The harder I tried, the harder it became. The moth drew closer to the light.

The minister's voice a soft hiss in the still air, I asked myself, is there a God?

Is there a God?

The question frightened me, although at that moment I had no way of knowing that I would not sit in that church again, that thirty years would pass before I'd find an answer for myself: *Is there a God?*

I waited.

Nothing.

Again I asked, is there a God?

No response.

I could stand it no longer. The moth dove into the flame. If there's a God, I prayed, strike me dead! I shuddered. Squeezing my eyes tightly shut, I awaited the worst.

Some seconds passed. I raised my right eyelid slightly. Through the haze I saw heads bobbing.

I opened both eyes wide. I was safe! The moth had escaped

the flame uncharred and knew that it was stronger than before.

When I prayed again, it was with more, not less, confidence: I don't know whether you're there, God, but I do know what I'm going to do. No matter how I'm punished, I'm not going through with confirmation. If you exist, don't stop me. *Don't bother me; I won't bother you.* That's the deal — and if you don't exist, none of this matters, does it?

The next hour stands out as one of the most anxious of my childhood. The walk home was not long enough. I couldn't seem to get my thoughts together. I knew I had to tell my parents I was not going to be a Lutheran — this, after they had spent money, money we didn't have, to send me to a parochial school. What would I say? What would they say? Or do? I was sure my mother would listen, but my father . . . well, I didn't know. Would I be beaten? Would I be told I *had* to go through with the confirmation? I feared that most of all. I could take the beating; I could not be confirmed. I would not.

For several seconds I stood in front of the door to our apartment. *What am I going to do?*

When I finally walked in, my mother was setting the table for dinner.

"Hi, honey," she said.

"Hi, Mom. Where's Daddy?"

"Sleeping."

"I've got something I want to say." She stopped. "It's this: I don't want to be confirmed in that church. I don't believe any of it, Mom . . ."

I continued at length, honestly answering the questions she raised, leaving out only the part about asking God to strike me dead.

My mother was quiet for a few minutes.

"Are you sure?" she asked, her decision made.

"I really am."

"Let me talk to your father first," she told me.

"What do you think he'll say?"

"He'll support you."

"He will?"

"Yes, he will."

"How can you be so sure?"

"I'm sure."

She was right.

My father, to my relief, was matter-of-fact, neither angry nor pleased — and he also asked me, "Are you sure?"

When I told him I was, he said, "Then that's your decision."

The next morning, when I asked to speak with the minister, I was more nervous than I had expected to be.

Did I say nervous?

I was scared.

"Reverend," I stammered, "I don't want to be confirmed."

"Why?" he asked, his eyebrows raised as if he had heard a strange sound from another room.

I hesitated. Remembering my vow, I steeled myself.

"I don't believe —" I began.

"— in *God?*" he interrupted, his eyes widening.

"— in what I've been taught," I said.

He was a kind, sympathetic man, and he talked for a solid ten minutes, repeatedly assuring me that doubt was not unusual.

I listened respectfully.

Finally he asked, "Are you sure?"

"Yes, sir," I said.

"Maybe next year," he told me.

I don't think I ever saw him again.

Whether we feel frightened or only vaguely uneasy in the face of a risk, it's critical to be honest, to ask, what am I responding to? Whom am I trying to please?

I know now that my decision in that church thirty years ago was as hard a choice as I've ever had to make; I know also that the way in which a child interprets a parent's action, as you'll see in the experience of the remarkable leader we're about to meet, can be more important than the action itself.

Her childhood, she told me, was like walking along a six-lane highway when everyone else was riding by in cars. Her family was led by a father who ran a resort in summer and roamed from coast to coast selling antiques in winter. Her parents divorced when she was eleven, and she was left to care for her emotionally fragile mother in a pest-infested house in a decaying neighborhood in Toledo. The following year, when she was twelve, she attended a full term of school for the first time — but she was an inexperienced student, and, plump and different-seeming, she was not popular. Having lived almost exclusively in the company of adults, she had little experience with other children. Then her mother's mental illness worsened.

Life toughened.

If only that lonely child somehow could have known that one day she would be recognized throughout the world; that she would be respected for her intellect, her will, her kindness, her integrity; that she would be called *beautiful*; that she would graduate with high honors from Smith College and later be named a Woodrow Wilson International Scholar. In years to come she was to write several books, including the best-selling *Outrageous Acts and Everyday Rebellions*, and help start two important magazines, *New York* and *Ms*. A crusader, she'd campaign for scores of causes and be active in numerous political drives, but it was to be one cause, one movement, for which she became known best. For many, Gloria Steinem is its symbol.

As we sat facing each other in a small book-lined room off

the lobby of the Waldorf-Astoria in Manhattan one June morning in 1987, she spoke softly, reflecting on the questions I was asking about her childhood.

"What were you most afraid of?" I asked.

"Being all alone," she told me, "being on the fringe of life, having to do everything myself, not having anyone to take care of me. Actually, I feared precisely what I was experiencing."

"Were you lonely?"

"Yes," she said. "I was different from other children in that I had not regularly attended school, and after my parents separated, I had to look after my mother. There were times when my mother seemed to be in another world, and she could be very difficult to control, especially when I was a small child. Thus, the hardest memories of my childhood are of how alone I felt when I was with my mother. When I was by myself, I was less alone, less lonely, than when I was with her — and it was a luxury when I had a break, those times when I did not have to care for her."

No one person, I knew, can found a movement. Nevertheless, once Gloria was involved, her participation in the women's movement — which was as intense and as visible as that of leaders like Betty Friedan, Bella Abzug, or the Australian feminist Germaine Greer — made her the living example of feminism to millions, and to some the ideal. I recalled the story of her fortieth birthday party thirteen years earlier, when a reporter had told her, "You don't look forty," and her reply, "But this is what forty looks like. We've been lying so long, who would know?" Well, I noted, fifty-three looked terrific. She wore a plain black blouse and a tan skirt, only a dusting of makeup and no lipstick, no earrings, a simple gold watch on her wrist, and a gold ring cut into the design of a coiled snake. She was slender, and her light brown hair, neatly parted in the center, was cut long to frame her delicate face. Her large brown eyes were warm and friendly.

"You didn't do well in school?" I asked.

She shook her head.

"Why?"

"Partly because I wasn't able to attend class regularly," she explained. "As I've said, I didn't go to school much until I was twelve years old. And partly because doing poorly was socially rewarded."

"Socially rewarded?"

"Yes," she replied. "Because I had lived all my early years traveling around the country with adults, I spoke with a grown-up vocabulary — and I'm sure I was offensive to kids my age. Also, though I had made some individual friends here and there, I had no experience playing with other children in a group. When I was twelve, I had to learn quickly. I soon discovered that to be too smart, to know too many words, was not good. So I played it down. Then, later, teenage girls were supposed to be feminine, and that was seen as the opposite of smart."

"What was your high school like?"

"I attended a big midwestern working-class high school, where most of the boys started working in the factories right after graduation — if they hadn't already quit to work in the factories at sixteen. Girls married young, often because they were pregnant. Sometimes they worked for a little while in the gas company or the phone company, but the point was to get married. That's what life was. I left during my senior year and went to live with my sister in Washington."

"How did adults act?"

"You know about my mother. My father had two points of pride: He never wore a hat; he never held a job. He meant, when he boasted like that, that when he worked, he worked for himself, whether it was operating summer resorts or selling antiques. Many of my friends' parents were Polish or Hungarian and were not only illiterate in English but in their native languages as well. What was rewarded was hard work, bringing home the paycheck. I didn't know many people, aside from teachers, who read books, who thought about ideas. Grown-ups, I learned, worried about tangible things: Does your husband beat you up on Saturday night? Is your mother-in-law sleeping on your couch?"

"How did you feel?"

"I thought I was peculiar. Ideas mattered to me. I escaped into books, into fantasy, into some other life. I lived somewhere inside my head. When I was with strangers, I tried to be charming. I wanted to be liked. So I played down my vocabulary, my reading."

"Were you attractive?"

"No, I was plump — not unpretty, but ordinary. My whole family struggles with weight. My father spent most of his life weighing more than three hundred pounds."

"Did you feel loved as a child?"

"Yes. Unlike others who've had hard, insecure childhoods, I'm not angry at my parents. I understand that they did the best they could with what they had to give."

She paused.

"Walter," she said, "I think that's all any child wants to know. My parents treated me better than, or at least as well as, they treated themselves. I think kids know when their parents are doing the best they know how. A lot of bad things occurred in my childhood, and honestly, I haven't embraced it all yet. But I don't feel angry toward my parents. And that's because I've always known that they loved me."

"Have you found real security?"

"Yes," she said, "I have by trying to face the worst that can happen. For years, whenever I'd pass a slum, especially any similar to the one in which I grew up, I'd imagine myself living there again — and I would wonder whether that's where I'd end up. Now I handle that fear by saying, 'So what? It's a life like any other. If I become a bag lady, I'll organize the other bag ladies.' Now please don't misunderstand. I am not flippant; this is serious for me. I do not want to end up on the street, and finally I'm trying to do something about it. Up until this year, anything I earned that was more than I needed to support myself, I gave away. On one level this was a rational decision, because I found it personally rewarding to see what good could come of the money I gave away —"

She took a deep breath, sat forward in her chair.

"— and on another level, I now realize, it was irrational, because I was replicating the way I grew up. Money was not familiar to me. How could I trust what I did not understand? The thought of money itself was scary — but really, I was just repeating the patterns of a neglected childhood, because it felt familiar, it felt like home. Money had its own weight; it had its own responsibility. Now, belatedly, I'm trying to save, to plan for the future.

"A conversation I had a couple of days ago with a friend, a very wise woman, is revealing. I just finished traveling across the country, I told her, and the people I met were extraordinary. Flight attendants would ask about the future of the Equal Rights Amendment, then try to slip me into first class or quietly smuggle a first-class dinner to me. A cleaning woman in one airport gave me her little closet to sleep in for three hours between flights. It made me believe, as Gandhi said, that if you do something that the people care about, the people will take care of you.

"When I finished saying all this to my friend, she responded:

" 'Gloria,' she said, 'but first, you have to be able to buy a plane ticket.'

"She's right, of course."

"Can a person change?" I asked.

"I think so," Gloria said, pausing as if searching for a memory.

"Yes." She began again, nodding.

"I changed. When I was in college, for example, I fell in love with conventionality. People lived in houses. They took naps; they had security. I fell in love with that life as only someone who has been deprived of it can. But then slowly I began to understand it was not real security after all."

"Did that understanding inspire you to take risks?"

"Yes," she said, "and I took big risks that I didn't see as risks. When I was twenty-two, just graduated from college, I was engaged to be married to a very nice man who was seven or eight years older than I. He was an interesting person, from a musical family — and I liked him a great deal. But I knew it would be a mistake for me to marry him. Also, I was independent in a sense, because my mother was in a mental hospital at the time, which meant travel for me was possible. About that time I received a thousand-dollar grant to study in India. I persuaded Pan Am to give me a free ticket by convincing them that I'd write something of merit. So there I was, totally alone in a foreign country with a thousand dollars to survive with. Now that was a large risk — but it seemed less of a risk than getting married at the time."

"Who inspires you?"

"Many people," she replied. "Bobby Kennedy, Bella Abzug, and Alice Walker, for example."

"How have they touched you?"

"Their courage has moved me. I try to remember Bobby Kennedy when I have to speak before a group. He and I used to talk about speaking in public, how frightening it was to both of us. Believe it or not, he was even more nervous than I am. Yet he did it. Also, I don't like to face conflict; it gives me a stomachache. That's where Bella inspires me. She's so courageous. She cares so much, she wades right in. As for Alice Walker, she may be the best writer alive, because she can empathize her way into any other person, and even into animals and trees."

"What have you feared most?"

"For years after *Ms.* magazine started, there were growing problems, hostilities and resentments, as well as great satisfactions. I hated the conflict. I found myself imagining a pleasurable fantasy: *Ms.* would burn down. A fire, an accident would not have been my fault — so, though the magazine would have closed, I would not have let women down. And with *Ms.* closed, people would like me again, because people like women who fail; they punish women who succeed. What I feared was not failure but humiliation."

"Gloria, have you ever asked, 'Is that all there is?' "

"Yes, but perhaps differently from what you might expect. I ran from my childhood, the poverty and the humiliation. I had no goals. And I was encouraged to think that I couldn't save myself; I'd have to marry someone who could save me. I didn't think about goals. Planning ahead is a measure of class. The degree to which you can control your future makes you aware of how much power you have. Rich people plan for three generations; poor people plan for Saturday night."

Clearly, our parents influence us, but — as we have seen with Carol Burnett, Jim Webb, and now Gloria Steinem — what happens outside our homes and inside our minds shapes us too. We are not condemned to hesitate, falter, or fail merely because we have done so before.

Remember, though, resolve is not enough. To change the way in which we perceive risks, we must not only understand how we've come to think as we do, but also identify the losses involved. When we cling to some false notion, however secure it makes us feel, we both retard our personal growth and make it far more difficult — and dangerous — to take a risk.

Ask, am I acting like a child?

Why?

Only I can change my life.

"Gloria," I asked at the end of our interview, "can we learn to take risks?"

"I believe we can," she said. "I think that's precisely what growing up is — steadily learning to take more and greater risks. While it's easy — and helpful — to see the facility for risk-taking grow in a child, it's important to remember that this process continues all our lives."

Part Two

ONE DAY, like an egg bursting from within, the shell of the child falls away. Suddenly there stands before us a human being who bristles with indignation, a moody stranger who can, at the slightest provocation, be intolerant, rebellious, rude, boastful, even deceitful. We call this season of our lives adolescence; for our parents, it's a lot like waltzing with a porcupine.

Only yesterday, it seems, we were looking to adults for approval and support. Now, in our teens, with the eggshell fragments of our childhood falling about us, we erupt. We're not sure whether we're good or bad, powerful or weak; whether we're men or boys, women or girls. Often we try to hide, with bluster and arrogance, the uncertainty we feel inside. Confused, depressed, often frightened, we may act selfish, distrustful, impetuous. On one hand, life's a joyous discovery, an awakening. On the other, it baffles and flusters. Pimples mottle our skin; hair sprouts in hidden places; our voices crack; erotic dreams disturb our sleep. We crave to understand, to control what's happening to us. Urgently we ask, who are we?

The question, of course, pops up throughout our lives, but at no time do we seek the answer with more fervor, or with more reckless abandon — and never does the answer seem more elusive.

Who are we?

Children, as we discussed earlier, learn when to trust; adolescents search for identity. It's during our teenage years, as we begin our struggle to discover who and what we are, that our risks seem most chaotic. We dive into situations we're not quite ready to handle, and inevitably grope our way through one mess after another. Seeking control, often we're out of control. We live life in the extreme. We are either girls *or* women, boys *or* men, good *or* bad, superior *or* inferior — no shades of gray. We're convinced that no one, particularly not our parents, can understand what we're feeling. Thus we try to hide our terrible self-doubt. We deny our uncertainty; we speak with authority, *false* authority. We live in a world of worst and best.

Do you remember, *really* remember?

When we're teenagers, we undergo swift, radical change — and frequently we act out our confused emotions, renouncing loudly, unequivocally, any suggestion that threatens to reveal what we truly feel, the secret doubts we may have about ourselves. We're stuck on a speeding roller coaster, flailing about as we try to slow it, turn it, direct it, understand it.

Alone, we cry, what's happening to me?

We're growing up.

We're learning to think for ourselves; we're taking risks. Instinctively we push away the very people who are closest to us, who have been teaching us, caring for us, so that we can learn to draw our own conclusions. We experiment, with results that may be rewarding, may be comical, may be tragic.

Of course, adolescence does not stop like a clock at the end of our teen years. For most of us, this stage continues through our twenties — and for some, beyond. We've all known adults who try to hide what they really fear by taking risks that are clearly rash, reckless, self-destructive — people who take risks for all the wrong reasons, who antagonize, who posture, who greedily seek to acquire money or power yet never seem to have enough to feel satisfied, who display love flamboyantly yet never seem to like themselves, and who, whether their risks succeed or fail, never seem to learn from their experiences.

Childish?

No, *adolescent*.

That's why this stage of life is important. Often, when an adult is told he's acting like a child, he's not childish at all, but adolescent. We need to know the difference. Goaded by insecurity and fear of discovery, any one of us can act adolescent, though the body ages and the hair turns gray. Confidence, as I wrote earlier, comes from doing. We must take risks to know who we are. We only grow, though, when we take risks wisely — a lesson driven home to me late one spring evening on a Mount Vernon street corner.

I was fifteen, immersed in my own thoughts as I walked along Third Street. I was preoccupied because about an hour earlier I had witnessed an assault on a boy named Tony who was two years older than I. He had been jumped by five boys his age from the Wakefield section of the Bronx.

I knew Tony from Teen Town, which was a city-sponsored recreation center located on the second floor of a three-story building near the edge of the railroad cut that split Mount Vernon.

Tony — who was very muscular but moved, and maybe thought, a little slowly — had argued with one of the five (the leader, apparently) over whose turn was coming up at Ping-Pong. Actually it was Tony's turn, and the boy from the Bronx was trying to cut the line. Tony and the boy had rushed at each other after an exchange of words at the table, so a counselor, an adult in his forties, asked for identification from everyone involved, me first.

I showed him my card, loudly adding, "Eleventh and Third," which was where I lived.

"How about *you?*" the counselor demanded, turning to another teen.

"White Plains Road —" The boy had slipped, giving away that he lived in the Bronx.

"Teen Town is for Mount Vernon residents only," he was told flatly. "Out — *now.*"

With more than forty teenagers circling the counselor, and Tony still sizzling, the five Bronx boys left, of course amid catcalls.

"Seeya, *girls!*"

"Be good now."

"Don't go away mad," said one boy.

"Yeah," shouted another, "just go away."

"Yoo-hoo," a girl called after them, "we'll be seeing yoo-hoo."

They slowed at the foot of the stairs. The smallest of the five turned back, threatening, "Yeah, you will."

"*Ooooohhh,*" the crowd at the top of the stairs ridiculed in unison. Even the counselor laughed.

When Tony and I left Teen Town a half hour later, he proceeded to tell me how fortunate the boy from the Bronx had been. "That kid missed a real beating!" he insisted.

"Yeah," I agreed, "he was lucky."

Unfortunately, though, we were not.

"Hey!" a boy shouted as we passed a corner a block from Teen Town. "Wait up!"

Down the street, leaning on a black customized '49 Ford, were three of the teenagers from the Bronx. The others were sitting inside.

I wanted to run. We had time, because the boys, excited by spotting their quarry, had hailed us too quickly. Even though they had a car, I realized, Tony and I could escape if we charged for an alleyway across the street. They can't follow us between the buildings with their car, I silently reassured myself, and at nearly a quarter of a block away, neither can they catch us on foot. Good, I thought, we can outrun them.

"Want to make it?" I asked Tony.

"No," he said. "Let's get it on."

I felt my stomach tighten.

Looking back across the years, I see clearly that if Tony had been alone, he would have run. If I had been alone, I would have run. Together, though, we stood our ground, neither willing to admit fear to the other. So when Tony declared, "Let's get it on," I agreed.

"Yeah!" I said.

As the boys from the Bronx walked toward us, I noticed that the face of the tallest — the one Tony had argued with earlier — was curiously moist, glistening as if he had oiled his skin. It made him distinctive, as did his manner. Calm, smiling and friendly, when he spoke, his voice was soft, soothing.

"You want to finish it now?" he asked.

"Right now," Tony said, starting to slip out of his new powder-blue jacket.

The tall boy held up his hand, almost apologetically.

"No," he said quietly, "not here. This is just between you and me, not these guys or *him*" — he pointed to me, and my stomach tightened another notch — "just the two of us."

I could tell he had Tony's attention. He had everybody's attention.

On the surface, the boy from the Bronx didn't look like he could beat Tony. Although he was much taller and maybe a little heavier, Tony was as strong, as thick, as hard-muscled as a construction worker. When he wore a T-shirt, with one sleeve rolled up to hold his Lucky Strikes, you could see his arms, back, and chest rippling.

The settled confidence of the tall boy, though, was disconcerting. I could see the concern deepen in Tony's eyes. Too late, he realized the reality of what he was facing. The boy from the Bronx had four friends with him, all but one about his size, all his age. Tony had me, two years younger. Plainly we were in trouble.

Tony tried bluffing.

"You and me," he said slowly, gruffly.

The tall boy seemed to smile more widely, then he pointed toward a truck loading platform set between two buildings and across from some apartments.

"Over there?" he asked Tony.

The light from the streetlamps barely reached that far back. We could see, but it was dark and shadowy. I hoped no one would speak to me. I worried: Would my voice crack? I was frightened; I saw no way out.

"Good," Tony replied.

Stupid, I thought.

As we crossed the street, the boy from the Bronx, still smiling, casually changed the rules. He pointed to the shortest guy in his group.

"You and him," he said to me.

I nodded.

Although the boy was about my height, he was at least two or three years older, and much heavier and stronger. If I could have bolted, I would have. Instead, trying to hide my fear, I looked hard into his eyes.

To my surprise, he looked away — but then he turned back and whispered, "Just you and me."

His hesitancy gave me hope. Maybe he didn't want to fight.

But if he does, I thought — and now my stomach tightened to a knot — I'm going to be hurt. How badly? Will my face be stomped? Does he have a knife, a sharpened belt buckle? Will I be cut? What can I do? I *can't* run. Maybe if these guys actually let us fight one-on-one, I can hit him quickly in the nose or kick him in the groin. Will he fall for a sucker punch? Who am I kidding? If I start to win, his pals will jump in. What am I going to do?

In my back pocket was a knife with a three-and-a-half-inch blade that sprang open when you pressed a button in the handle. I carried it for show, never intending to use it; I had bought it only a few days before from another boy at Teen Town for three dollars. I hadn't thought I could pull a knife ever, even to keep from getting hurt. Now I wasn't sure.

Tony and the boy from the Bronx, followed by three of his friends, climbed up onto the platform.

"Let's do it, man," the boy said, his hands rising to his lapels, as if he were going to take off his coat.

Tony, watching him, started to shrug his own jacket from his shoulders.

No, I thought, don't!

Too late.

When Tony's jacket dropped to his elbows, the other boy, his coat still in place, slugged Tony. Quickly one of the others grabbed Tony's jacket from behind. His large arms now bound in his own sleeves, straitjacketed, Tony cursed and struggled as the blows rained.

I froze.

The shorter boy, who had not mounted the platform with the others, glanced at me.

I didn't move.

He paused, then scrambled up onto the platform.

Tony was hunched over, trying to protect himself with his

back. He was too tightly centered in the group to fall. Laughing loudly, one of the kids swung a short emergency chain, probably stolen from a subway train; another used a garrison belt. Tony screamed curses.

"What's going on over there?" a voice yelled from one of the apartments. "Get out of there! I'm calling the cops!"

Still I stood entranced, unmoving, the world in slow motion. I heard the sound of a siren.

"Let's make it!" shouted the shiny-faced boy.

All five boys from the Bronx ran past me, shoving, laughing loudly, jeering, and Tony, still cursing, fell to the ground. I turned and saw the '49 Ford, its tires squealing, pull from the curb.

"It ain't done!" shouted one of the boys.

Tony, still cursing, shook his fist at them.

"How do I look?" he asked me.

The question snapped me back to full speed, normal. His left cheek was red and swollen; he'd have a black eye the next day. His lip was bleeding and he had a bruise and a small cut on his hairline, but all things considered, he was in good shape.

"You look okay," I said, then asked, "You all right?"

"I think so," he told me. "I don't think nothing's broke."

"Good," I said. "Let's go back to Teen Town and get you cleaned up."

"Okay," he agreed, then added angrily, "I'd like to get him back. He's yellow. I want to fight him one-on-one."

"Right," I said, though I knew that if Tony fought that boy a thousand times, he'd lose a thousand times. Tony was too slow, thinking and moving. The other boy, a classic bully, knew it.

I wanted to tell Tony I was sorry for doing nothing.

But I didn't.

Instead I listened quietly to Tony's angry threats as we

walked back to Teen Town, where a counselor, quickly surrounded by teenagers, helped clean Tony up.

"What happened?" the counselor asked.

"We were jumped," Tony said.

"How come *you* ain't hurt?" somebody asked me.

I ignored the question.

"How come?"

Tony, thinking I didn't hear, volunteered, "He was wrestling around with the short guy."

He believed I had!

"Yeah," I lied, relieved that no one would know that I had frozen, that I had *chickened*. "They really wanted Tony, but Tony fought like hell," I exaggerated, my tone grave. "He fought four of them. I just had the one."

"Did you get him?" someone asked me.

"I don't think I really hurt him," I replied, secretly noting to myself, at least that's true.

Tony relished the attention. His fellow teenagers fired questions; they all admired him for fighting off four guys — and luckily, he had a witness to confirm his courage: me.

Later I walked alone along Third Street, immersed in my own thoughts. I was disturbed, on one hand, by what I perceived as my cowardice, but relieved, on the other, that no one knew my secret.

I passed the poolroom not far from my home and nodded to the older brother of a high school classmate of mine, a boy nicknamed Slim, who was standing in the doorway. He nodded back.

Recognition was important along Third Street, a few short blocks that beat with the clank of metal parts and the din of human voices and the squealing of tires and the sounds of breaking glass. It was a lively avenue that had the smells, fresh and stale, and the colors, from dull rust to fluorescent violet, of several bars, two poolrooms, some gas stations, a fish market, various dry cleaning, grocery, and liquor stores, storefront churches, barber shops, walk-up tenements, and public housing projects. Good people lived here, sometimes only a thin plaster wall away from those who were not. Teenagers sang *a cappella* on the corners, songs made famous by such groups as the Platters, the Dimensions, the Shirelles, and, of course, Mount Vernon's own Mello Kings. Basketball was played seriously on nearby playgrounds, and sometimes raised to high art in bruising, brilliant games. A candy store was a bookie joint where many, like my father, bet the daily numbers. Drunks, usually harmless, bobbed along late at night. A siren could signal a robbery, a rape, a birth, a death. Third Street, with all its extremes, was a patchwork, a community unto itself. You were part of the neighborhood, or you were not.

I belonged.

Thus I was surprised when, still deep in a cloud, I heard someone ask, "Where you goin'?"

I looked up. The voice belonged to a shiny face. Because I had been walking with my head down, distracted, I hadn't noticed the '49 Ford at the curb across the street. I realized instantly: They had heard me answer "Eleventh and Third" when I was in Teen Town!

"Where's your man?" the boy from the Bronx asked, referring to Tony.

"I don't know," I said.

"Where's he live?"

"I don't know."

Could they hear my heart? *I* could hear it. Please, I prayed, don't let my voice squeak.

"I'm gonna ask you again, four-eyes, where's he live?"

"Don't know." My voice cracked.

The boy from the Bronx placed his hand on my chest and

pushed me back hard. I stumbled against a chain link fence, the back of my skull cracking against it.

He laughed.

Cocky, toying with me as his friends giggled, he didn't notice my right hand sliding into my back pocket.

I could threaten — I could show my knife . . . or I could use it. I felt my neck and cheeks redden.

He put his finger on my chest.

"Where?" he asked.

"Don't know," I repeated, my voice harder, deeper, this time not cracking. It was as if a feather that had been tickling my stomach suddenly turned to flame. I had been humiliated; I was angry.

He dropped his hand and backed away, sensing *something*.

I pledged silently: Punk, you'll bleed tonight. I squeezed the knife in my hand, my thumb on the button.

"I think you —" he started, stepping toward me again, but before he could finish he was interrupted.

"The man *said* he didn't know."

I was startled. The voice was Slim's, and the change in the air was sudden, like a motion picture abruptly stopping, snapping an audience to attention. Behind Slim stood several Majestic Lords, a gang with many members on Third Street. Though Slim wasn't a member, the Majestic Lords were among his friends.

The boy from the Bronx had a pained expression, like Tony had had earlier, as if he'd eaten something sour.

I had seen Slim fight only once, outside the poolroom, with an adult, a street tough who had instigated the quarrel. Slim's younger brother, Billy, and I watched him hit the man smoothly, cleanly, moving like a professional fighter. The fight ended in less than a minute, with Slim on top. Everyone who watched — and it was the talk of the neighborhood at the time — knew that Slim could not only box, he could box well.

Glancing around, the other boys from the Bronx looked like they had eaten the same bad food as the boy with the shiny face. Their leader now tried to bluff: "This ain't your business."

"What ain't my business?" Slim asked.

"Him," the boy said, pointing to me. "This is between me and him."

"*Him*," Slim said, "is my baby brother."

One of the Lords chuckled. I was very white; Slim was very black.

"He's not —" But the boy stopped short of calling Slim a liar.

"Not *what?*"

The boy said nothing.

A neighborhood crowd started to form.

"Hey, Slim, give him a whipping," someone shouted out.

"Yeah, yeah, whip him," another followed.

Slim only turned once to the crowd, his face serious. No one made any more suggestions.

I still held my knife tightly.

The short boy said, "Let's get out of here."

"Get in your car," Slim ordered.

"*Ooohhh*," someone moaned in the crowd, disappointed.

I loosened my grip.

The five started to cross the street, but Slim stopped the boy with the shiny face.

"Not *you*," he said.

The boy looked awful.

"You got to pay a toll."

The boy looked worse.

Slim spoke softly, menacingly, to the four: "Just so you understand. I'm telling you I'm going to talk a little to your chief here. If you want to get into the conversation, they" — he signaled to the Lords — "will hear you out."

Slim slapped the boy. It was so sudden that no one, least of all the boy from the Bronx, expected it.

"Can you hear me better now?" Slim asked.

The boy glowered.

"I don't want no trouble," he said, turning away. But spinning quickly, he tried to land a punch.

Slim seemed to step to the side, and the boy missed completely and stumbled, twisting sideways. Slim slapped him again.

"Don't come back," Slim said, faking another slap. When the boy raised his hands, falling for the feint, Slim punched him in the stomach.

"Hear me?"

The boy, gasping, nodded.

"Take him home," Slim told the others, none of whom had moved since the first slap.

Amid catcalls and challenges from the Lords, the five quietly got into their car. Not a word. Not even a mean look. Then, as the car drove away, it slowed, and the five shouted curses back.

One Majestic Lord suggested, "Stay around. We'll *talk* some more."

Several people on the street burst into laughter.

The car sped off and the crowd dispersed, leaving Slim and me, me still shaken. I thanked him. He shook his head.

"I was scared," I admitted, surprised that I said it, not knowing why I said it.

"Five to one, even punks like that, you'd be a fool not to be scared."

I nodded.

"Why didn't you run or yell?"

"They surprised me."

"That's dumb."

Agreeing, I nodded again. "I'm really glad you helped me out."

"If it wasn't me, it would have been them" — he looked toward two of the Majestic Lords — "or some of the men. No one can come here and take a kid out like that. Nobody should ever surprise you in your own neighborhood. *You weren't even in trouble.* All you had to do was yell."

"I know," I said. "I wasn't paying attention."

"Pay attention!" he told me, his voice sharp. "Next month you won't have me around to get you and Billy out of trouble."

"Where you going?"

"The Marines."

"You got in?"

"Yeah."

"That's great. Billy told me you were going to enlist, Slim. Hey, good luck!"

"Thanks," he said, then added, "one more thing —"

"Yeah?"

"What did you have in your pocket before?"

I showed him my knife.

"Get rid of it," he ordered.

I nodded.

"I'm not kidding," he said.

I nodded again.

"Now take off," he told me, laughing, "before Mom gets worried."

To my surprise, when I told Tony what had happened the following afternoon, he was more impressed that Slim was going into the Marines than he was with the fight.

"I'm going to be a Marine too!" he declared.

"You are?"

"Yeah."

"Why?" I asked.

"They're the baddest," he told me, adding somberly, "and everybody respects 'em!"

"Really?"

"Man," he said, "Parris Island boot camp is bad news — but I'll make it. I do a lot of pushups. Yeah, I'm going in the Marines too."

Let's examine the risks blindly taken by these teenagers. Although Tony recognized that he couldn't emerge from the fight safely, he proceeded anyway. He knew we could not win; I knew we had no chance. Clearly, Tony and I risked our well-being out of fear, the naked fear of two adolescents who were more worried about being embarrassed than about being hurt. Fight *four*? Tony, despite his strength, would have struggled to survive one — and I was so terrified I froze. The boy from the Bronx wisely assessed his chances, and he proceeded calmly — though his quick and early success led him (as often occurs in adolescence) to overconfidence. Thus emboldened, he failed to perceive that he and his small group would be seriously at risk in my neighborhood.

When I clutched my knife, what did I risk? If I stabbed the boy, there was a chance, however small, that in the confusion I might escape his friends. More likely, I would not. Whatever the outcome, it would have been fairly easy for the Mount Vernon police to find the teenager from Eleventh and Third, particularly given my description and the earlier incident near Teen Town. I'm sure I would have been arrested, and possibly found guilty of illegal weapon possession, assault — maybe worse. In a second, perhaps a fraction of a second, my life would have been altered forever. Fortunately, I was given another chance. Slim settled that — and he also taught me an important lesson: *I wasn't even in trouble.* Humiliated, I hadn't noticed. I wrongly perceived both the risk and the answer to it. If I had yelled, of course someone would have helped me. I had clasped the knife in anger, not in self-defense. I had only wanted to strike out: "Punk, you'll bleed tonight."

I share such a violent and painful memory precisely because at first reading it may appear to be little more than an interesting exception. It's easy to think, this could not happen to me. Few risks we face as adolescents seem on the surface to be so filled with danger, but I suspect that far more teens die as their bodies explode through car windshields than at the edge of a knife — and as a journalist I've seen hundreds of lives end from drugs and alcohol. "Let's go for a ride!" and "Try these!" can be invitations as fraught with peril as "Let's get it on!" Too many adolescents die, some as suicides, because, like me against the fence, they respond inappropriately. Searching for their identity while trying to win the approval of their peers, they don't see the danger — *it won't happen to me.*

Consider again Carol Burnett's choice about ending her popular television series, the injury that finished Jim Webb's military career, the potential alienation Gloria Steinem faced because of her responsibility to *Ms.* magazine. Remember for a moment the self-doubt I felt the Sunday morning I sat in Immanuel Evangelical Lutheran Church, confused and agitated as I questioned the existence of God. The four of us prevailed in these instances because we responded not to our worst fears but to the *cause* of those anxious feelings — the risk at hand. Carol could have been forgotten. Jim could have been rejected. Gloria's magazine could have failed. I could have been ostracized for refusing to be confirmed a Lutheran.

Rejection, which was the risk we all shared, is never more terrifying than in adolescence. Carol, Jim, Gloria, and I, in the examples I've just cited, opened ourselves to the possibility of hurt. I'm sure that when I was a teenager I would have been surprised, if not flabbergasted, to be told that one day, *today*, I would write with conviction that vulnerability can make me stronger. I know now, though, that the approval of someone else is truly satisfying only when I've risked being rejected as I really am. Every time we're accepted by others after disclosing what we truly feel, one more brick is firmly cemented into the building of our personalities. Only by taking risks, by exposing ourselves to embarrassment, do we grow stronger, tougher, better able to handle being rejected. Ironically, often what we fear most when we're adolescents is the very process by which we learn to deal with rejection: *By revealing ourselves, we gain the true confidence that comes only from being accepted as we really are.*

But who are we?

If we programmed a supercomputer to calculate the precise number of raindrops in a mud puddle formed at our feet this afternoon, undoubtedly the machine would arrive at a number — perhaps even the correct number. It would know *something*. But would it know the water like the raccoon who sips at its edge or the toddler who splashes through it? I don't think so. The puddle is more than the sum of its drops; we are more than the sum of our experiences. It is true that we need others to help us explore our identities, but finally, each of us must answer alone the question "Who am I?"

I believe I can know myself three ways:

What I am.
What I have.
What I seem to be.

How we respond to each of these perceptions helps us to define our personalities.

What I am is who I am when I am alone, my inner self, the

whole complex framework of my abilities (both inherited and learned), my feelings, my fantasies, my desires. It is, as I will describe at some length later in this book, my essence.

What I have is my possessions, all that I own. Clothes tear, though. Houses age. Cars rust. Fortunes rise and fall. I think a religious anecdote I once heard best illustrates the fragile nature of what we believe we possess:

Noting the meager possessions of a wise and famous rabbi — and deeply disappointed by the simple manner in which the rabbi lived, despite his worldwide acclaim — a tourist rudely inquired, "Sir, is this all you have?"

The rabbi smiled, pointed to the tourist's suitcase, and asked, "Is that all *you* have?"

"Of course," insisted the tourist, "but I'm only passing through."

The rabbi nodded.

"So am I," he said.

What I seem to be is the opinion of me held by others. Seeing ourselves through the eyes of someone else, though, is more delicate, and often less sensible, than holding our possessions too tightly. As an editor, for example, how might I be described by the author whose manuscript I accept, by the author whose work I reject? Is one view more accurate than the other? As a father, how am I regarded by my children when I say yes, when I say no?

Invariably, adolescents seek to find themselves both in their possessions — notice the sudden interest in clothes! — and, with even more intensity, in the approval of their peers. With this in mind, let's examine the thoughtful experience of a prominent columnist who could not distinguish herself, could not soar, until she was able to distinguish *What I am* from *What I have*.

*

She had been a typist and she had sold hearing aids and she had been an associate producer at NBC, an editor at *Cosmopolitan* magazine, the author of *The Mother Book*, a staff writer for *Sports Illustrated*, a local television personality in New York — and at sixty-four she had written one of the most widely read, popular daily features in America for more than a decade. As we sat facing each other at a corner table of the Marco Polo Club in the Waldorf-Astoria one spring night in 1987, I recalled the day six years earlier when I had first met Liz Smith, whose enormously successful gossip column originates in the *Daily News* and is syndicated to more than sixty other newspapers across the country. My first three impressions of this talented woman, I realized, had been reinforced through the years. She was courteous, for one. Although our initial meeting had been at The Four Seasons during a luncheon overflowing with celebrities, Liz had spoken with me as if I were the only person in the room. Second, I was moved by her enthusiasm; it was clear this woman appreciated all she had earned. Third, she was kind. Liz told no mean stories about human failure, although she must hear scores of such tales every week.

This evening she wore a blue wool blazer over a pale yellow cotton blouse, with a smart black, red, and white designer scarf neatly tucked about her neck. Her earrings were small gray ceramic and silver circles, and she had a white bone and silver bracelet clasped on one wrist, a simple gold watch with a black lizard band on the other. Her cheeks were smooth and creamy, and her blond hair was carefully combed, straight, and full. I mention these details only to draw a coal in the snow — because amid these colors, it was Liz Smith's electric blue eyes — joyous, inquisitive eyes, the lively eyes of a curious child — that gave her presence.

I had looked forward to this dinner for some time, because

I hoped to find Liz's secret: Why do so many people open up to her, tell her the truth, share intimacies with her? I suspected it had something to do with that presence of hers, her openness. She was, I realized, one of the most likable people I had ever met. Effortlessly, it seemed, she projected love.

"Were you," I asked, "a risk-taker as a child?"

"Without a doubt," she said, laughing. "When I was a little girl, I was allowed to do nothing but take risks. My brothers made me put on wings and jump off the garage. They forced me to ride a bike when my feet could not reach the pedals. I loved them both, one older, one younger. I was the filling in their sandwich. They urged me, as brothers will, to do horrible little things. I loved it! I had a very daring childhood, believe me. I'm lucky I survived."

"Are you brave?"

"Not at all. Actually, I think of myself as a devout coward. On my own, I think, I'd do much less."

"What has moved you?"

"I highly recommend having other people in your life who prod you on to greater things — because you can react against what's wrong for you, and you can benefit from what's right. Early on, I worked as an assistant to some very famous men, like Mike Wallace, Allen Funt, Charles Saxon, who became the great *New Yorker* cartoonist, and Igor Cassini."

"Do you see anything in common among the famous people you write about in your column?"

"Only that they divide themselves into two groups: those who become famous overnight, and those who struggle for years. When acclaim comes instantly for the young, I've seen disaster overwhelm the rewards. John Belushi's a good example. How could he possibly have known who he was or what he would have liked to be? Then there are people like Barbara Walters, who has worked hard all her life, very hard, to be where she is. No instant glory there. I suspect Barbara probably had normal ambitions, but she's so extremely dedicated that finally, for her, the jackpot paid off. People like Barbara seem to enjoy themselves more; they have more fun with their success. Call it confidence. It's far more difficult for the young to grapple with attention, no matter how intensely they desire fame."

"How did you respond when you were younger?"

Her blue eyes widened, and she sat quietly for several seconds.

"That's a good question," she said, breaking the silence.

I sat quietly, waiting.

"When I was young," she began, "I was sexually precocious. I was cute and I was driven. I think I sought in sex a kind of identity and power. Today I have that in my work. Does that make sense at all?"

"Yes, but what changed?"

"After I experienced legitimate success, I was less driven and insecure. I had been flailing, striving with no real purpose or direction. I didn't know who I was or who I wanted to be."

She paused.

"I wanted *everything*. I spent all those early years in New York having a wonderful time — and still wanting. Wanting to be invited to every party, wanting to wear great clothes, to go to Europe, to speak six languages, to sleep with everyone."

"Then?"

"After I felt real success, it seemed I was driven less by sex and its pointless substitution for force and power. Now I wonder if our sex drive doesn't compensate at times for our insecurity, whether we don't act out sexually far deeper needs. Getting older has been wonderful. I'm far more able to be friends with men; I do not have to analyze my effect on them sexually, or my lack of effect. Don't misunderstand — I want to be attractive. But I understand now there's more. For a woman to be friends with a man is both liberating and exhilarating. Women do not have to lose their sexuality to be friends with men. As I've grown in this understanding, Walter, I've found something important. I've found *me*. And I like me as an adult, as a real person, as a true friend, much better. I think other people do too."

"When did you start to really know yourself?"

"Let me tell you a story that was a revelation to me. For years, as I worked variously for Igor Cassini, Allen Funt, Mike Wallace, and NBC's Norman Frank, I was a first-rate person's second person. Much of the work I did as an assistant involved complex projects. The filming of *Wide Wide World* for Norman Frank and Barry Wood, for example, required multiple broadcast facilities all over the world. I was usually very good in my Girl Friday job, but I found I was secretly sometimes delighted — delighted! — to present my bosses with problems, things that could not be done. I was eager to describe the problem — eager, in other words, to lay an insoluble problem at the foot of a busy man. Deep down I was jealous, maybe, of their fame or their power or their money. Yet it was amazing how many times they would in a positive way solve the problems, and never be angry with me."

She paused.

"Please," I encouraged.

"And one morning, as I realized I was about to enjoy telling someone important what could not be accomplished, I asked myself, 'Why do I take pleasure in this?' Then I asked, 'Do I like these people?' I did! They were very kind to me. I wanted them to succeed, because on top of everything else, their success would be my success."

She paused again.

"And in that moment, one career life ended and another

began for me, Walter. When I began sincerely to want others to succeed, when I worked to help them do just that, I quit being a second-rate assistant; I was no longer somebody's 'girl' but a true associate. And my career took off. Real success followed."

"Liz," I said, "I once heard you describe your childhood in Fort Worth as a tug-of-war between the Travis Avenue Baptist Church and the Tivoli movie theater. Do you still have that struggle?"

She laughed.

"Yes," she said, "but I believe God has to be greater than the finite idea of him as a punisher. I think a force greater than we are created human beings, because we all have impulses to be creators ourselves. Whenever man reaches his sublime, his divine reality, he creates something wonderful — an act of love or a wonderful painting or a feat of mind like Einstein's, the kind of overreaching that caused man in such a short time to scratch out of the mud and go to the stars. There just seems to be no limit to what man can do — and there are no depths to which he cannot plunge. Isn't this, though, what makes us different from other animals? We have the potential for good *and* evil. I don't think it makes much difference whether or not we consider ourselves floating in an endless void, either. Personally, I'd rather explore man's divine aspects. The nobility of the human being, I fully recognize, has been great in history, and yet so has the devastation mankind has wreaked. This is an imperfect world, but it has the capacity for beauty as well as ugliness."

She sat quietly. When she spoke again, her voice was firm.

"Every day of my life," she said, "I get up and go into the shower and I stand there and think about the Jews who had to get up and begin their slavery during the Holocaust. I don't know why this comes to mind every morning, but it does. I'm in a warm shower and I imagine how they had to work in freezing cold in little thin shirts and struggle to escape being killed. Their goal might be to survive two more weeks, or to find the strength to survive another day, because they knew they were systematically being starved to death. I don't know why I think about this. Perhaps it's an epiphany for me. Maybe it's my prayer.

"As I said earlier, I was extremely involved with love and romance when I was younger, and I rushed like a mad person trying to resolve my conflicts — but now I think the greatest thing that has happened to me is the wonderful friends I've made along the way. They are people I can really count on. This is the love that's really important. I had to be older, to have lived my life, to come to this truth. I was very involved with romantic love for years, but I don't think romantic relationships, as exciting as they are at first, last as we might wish. The great marriages, I believe, are those in which the partners become friends."

"How do you see risk today?"

"Ah-hah!" she replied, laughing. "Finally, an easy question."

"Give it a try!"

"If you don't place your foot on the rope, you'll never cross the chasm. Life is a risk. Change and chance are constants. The other night I watched Bette Davis perform, and I thought at first, she's making herself look like a fool. Then I realized the misunderstanding was mine, not hers. She's no fool. It's just that she doesn't look like she used to, the way she did when she was young, before a stroke and a mastectomy. I watched her and I realized this woman's not going to lie down. She is great, truly great. What risk she faces! She *dares* to be old, to be drawn, to be thin. While I was admiring her courage, the truth came to me. We should appreciate the reality that she's alive, that she's the way she is, that she has steadfastly refused to be carted off to a home somewhere, that she's here for all of us. What guts! What an example. She is, I realized, beautiful.

"I remember when my grandmother was eighty-two; she had saved her money and she made us drive her to the airport in Fort Worth. For five dollars you could go up in a plane. She said she had to have this experience before she died. We all stayed on the ground and we watched her. It was the Depression, and no one else had five dollars. I thought it was great that she did that. I was proud of her; she was a wonderful woman. Her name was Sally Ball McCall; she always told us she was kin to the Ball who had been related to George Washington."

Liz's blue eyes were bright, proud. She has, I knew, a lot of Sally Ball McCall in her. And I knew something else. Liz Smith has found joy in a profound way, outside of herself, in sharing. What she gives is what she receives.

What I am; what I have; what I seem to be.

As Liz Smith discovered, which of these three we're most eager to take a risk for — which is important to us — is a sure gauge of our maturity. Let's hear now from one of the wisest risk-takers I have known, a gentleman who is above all himself.

His office is on the third floor of a tall building at Columbus Avenue and Sixty-Seventh Street in Manhattan, and on a summer morning in 1987 it was brightly lighted by two banks of windows with healthy green floor plants at their sills. An ambitious young accountant might work here, or an executive on the rise; the work space, like its occupant, is open, meticulous, precise. Books, some he's written, neatly line the shelves along a beige wall. An American flag stands tall in one corner. No ragged typed sheets, no mounds of mail clutter his polished, modern oak desk. Its shiny top, I noted, was clear, clean, and —

like the television personality Hugh Downs, whose desk it is — *ready*.

I knew that Hugh had started at age eighteen in 1939 as a radio announcer in Lima, Ohio, for $12.50 per week, and that his first major television assignment had been in Chicago with the puppet show *Kukla, Fran & Ollie*, followed by the *Home* show in New York with Arlene Francis, *Caesar's Hour* with Sid Caesar, the *Tonight* show with Jack Paar, the *Today* show (where he met and encouraged a talented young writer by the name of Barbara Walters), the quiz show *Concentration*, and, of course, the popular report he joined in 1978 and now co-hosts with Barbara, *20/20*. Counting all these, he has appeared for more than ten thousand hours on commercial network television — more, as recorded in the *Guinness Book of World Records*, than anyone else.

Now, as he sat next to me, at ease on his beige couch and awaiting my first question, I remembered what Barbara, who had introduced us at a birthday party three years earlier, had told me about her long-time friend: "You can only do what Hugh has done when you have an inner security. He's the nicest, most thoughtful man in the business — kind, generous, and stable, a contradiction in that he's so outwardly calm, yet truly he has done the most daring things."

Hugh Downs, sixty-six as we spoke, has flown planes and gliders, scuba dived, ridden killer whales at Sea World in San Diego and Orlando, endured a grueling trek in the subzero temperatures of Antarctica so that he could move the bamboo marker at the South Pole to a more accurate position, successfully navigated a sailboat through high seas from Panama to Tahiti, and even driven a race car at the Indianapolis Motor Speedway and in the inaugural race at California's Ontario Speedway, where he placed fourth, winning his only sports trophy. But to my mind, what tops it all is two crucial risks

he has tackled: At the height of his career, Hugh Downs walked
away. Then he came back.

I hoped he'd talk about it.

"Hugh," I began, "after nine successful years on the *Today*
show, you resigned, gave it up for the Arizona desert, to teach
and to write —"

He nodded.

"— and seven years later, when *20/20* was foundering, ridiculed by the critics, you returned."

"Yes, that's true."

"Why?" I asked.

He nodded again and started to speak slowly, clearly, his
tone warm, instructive, like that of a friendly teacher: "It comes
partly, I think, from a desire — and I'm not sure where I got
this idea — to report to myself every decade. What troubled
me was not that my situation grew stale; it grew *comfortable*.
I left because I was in a rut, not having to exert myself. I felt
no anxiety, no adrenaline. It was, I knew, time to shake things
up. I had been on the staff of NBC for eleven years, did *Concentration* for ten years, *Today* for nine years."

"How long have you been with *20/20*?"

"Nine years," he replied, adding, "but I'm sure I'll sail
through my tenth year without feeling the need to do something different."

"Why?"

"I'm doing what I really want to do," he said, his smile
widening, "and there's nothing left in broadcasting that I consider up for me."

"What about anchor?"

"If ABC told me that Peter Jennings had decided to retire,
then asked me to succeed him, I'd say that I'm honored, but
I'd decline. I don't want to be corseted into the narrower format
of headline-type news. I've done a daily show and I know I

find news features more satisfying. In the past, when I've worked at something for about ten years — when I've no longer felt nervous — I've deliberately placed myself in a position in which I've had to take a gamble, as I did in Chicago when I left the security, the benefits, the solid retirement plans, and so on, when I chucked it all to go to New York."

"And *Tonight*?"

"When Jack Paar started with the *Tonight* show, it was a gamble for me, and after the first week both Jack and I thought the show became a parking lot — meaning it had few viewers — and that surely NBC would drop the show, run old movies in its place. But then, fortunately, *Tonight* took off."

"And *Today*?"

"*Today* was another gamble. Dave Garroway had been there for nine years, followed by John Chancellor, who desperately wanted to return to hard news. When NBC asked me to take over, the ratings and the revenues were zilch. What a risk! I remember thinking, 'Gee, if I ride this dog into the mire, the critics will skewer me, saying that Downs bit off more than he could chew.' But it worked out."

"Then the desert?"

He laughed.

"I decided to leave regular broadcasting," he said, "because I wanted to do some other things. I joined the faculty of Arizona State University, became a visiting fellow and later an adviser to the Center for the Study of Democratic Institutions. I joined the board of the National Space Institute, and when Wernher Von Braun, who became seriously ill, asked me to become president of the institute, I did — for six years."

"Did you expect the industry to call?"

"Yes."

"Did it happen?"

He shook his head.

"They did not beat a path to my door. Naively, I suppose, I expected all kinds of offers, calls like, 'Hugh, we want you for a ten-million-dollar special.' Instead I found a cliché to be true: 'Out of sight, out of mind.' I hadn't planned to quit. I had intended only to cut my workload, to pursue other interests, areas like aviation and wilderness experience."

"When did you realize what was happening?"

"In the early seventies, when I agreed to be a spokesman for Ford. I learned that Frank McGee had been sought for the job, but at the last moment he had to decline because of a contractual problem. I was told at a meeting, 'Hugh, we were casting about, desperate to find someone, then when your name came up, we all said *of course*, and wondered why we hadn't thought of you in the first place.' "

"Then you knew?"

"Yes, then I knew. I realized my problem was that they were not thinking of me first — or at all. Subsequently, I did a PBS series on aging, which — knock wood! — was successful. Not long after, ABC started *20/20*, and it was savaged, just torn apart by the critics. Then I was asked to be a host, which was agonizing."

"Agonizing?"

"Yes, *agonizing*. Making the decision to join *20/20* caused me the worst anguish of my career. I knew that this program, which was like *60 Minutes*, was the only project in broadcasting that could excite me — but quietly I had resigned myself, accepted years earlier that I'd never have the chance to do a show like that. Now, suddenly, one afternoon it was there. On one hand, I wanted the opportunity badly. On the other, it was frightening. *Twenty-twenty* seemed wrecked at that point; its reviews were scathing. If I took the risk, I could imagine how columnists would remind viewers that no one makes a comeback, citing people like Arthur Godfrey and Jack Paar. If I said yes, I knew that I'd have no fallback position. This was it. If *20/20* failed, I'd be discredited. I thought about my life, how fortunate I'd been, but I realized too that I didn't regret anything I'd done as much as what I'd not done. When I weighed the worst that could happen, I knew in a very personal way that I could carry a failure more easily than I could carry a missed opportunity. Then I felt, despite the odds, that I had to try. If *20/20* flopped, I suspect that I would have retreated, perhaps become reclusive. It was a tough decision, but I realized that if I walked away, I could not live with myself. What would I be feeling today if I had not taken that risk, had opted for the comfortable, and *20/20* had gone on to become as successful as it is without me?"

Hugh's brown eyes seemed to flicker as he spoke. They were warm and discerning, as open, as direct as his language. He leaned into his words, I noticed — ever the enthusiastic reporter. His dark blue suit was finely tailored, razor-creased, and his custom-made shirt was bright white, its French cuffs fastened by simple gold cufflinks, a crisp blue and white striped silk tie neatly knotted in its collar. Neat, I noted, like the man. If his were not one of the most famous faces in the nation, I wondered, what would he be? A pilot? A professor? An explorer? An agency president? Wait, he's done all that.

"Hugh," I asked, "have you always been a risk-taker?"

"No," he replied, shaking his head. "I was an extremely timid child. I was so timid I didn't play touch football, because I feared someone would bump into me."

"Do you recall the greatest risk you took as a child?"

"Yes," he said. "I desperately wanted to learn to swim, but I was terrified by the water. I remember the breakthrough, when I realized I could avoid sinking by my own actions! I had climbed a barrier. After that — simply floating — I learned to swim."

"Did you still fear the water?"

"Yes, most definitely. Even after I learned to swim, I had an inordinate fear of the water, particularly dark or angry water. I remember how one night when I was a young man, during a great, rampaging storm, I forced myself to walk to a little beach on the shore of Lake Michigan. Purposely, I stood on that beach while those waves crashed at my feet. I couldn't turn my back on it; I had to face my fear."

He paused, reflecting, seeming to collect words.

"Walter," he began again, "some years after the Michigan experience, when my son was four, we were vacationing at Banks Lake in Illinois. It is an east-to-west lake, shallow and long, and when an angry wind comes, a bad wave situation is created — worse, in fact, than anything I've experienced on the ocean. I was in a little boat with a tiny outboard motor, had no flotation compartments, stupidly, no life jackets. Suddenly the wind started to roar — and it was just my little son and me in this small boat. I saw that I could keep control of the boat if I kept the bow headed into the wind. But for fear of broaching or capsizing, I couldn't pay off to either side. I was sure I could swim to shore, but I didn't know if I could make it carrying my son, and of course I couldn't go without him."

He paused again.

"I was terrified. I could barely make headway. I couldn't get to the other end of the lake. I tried idling the motor, hoping the wind would blow us back to shore — and I began to lose control. *That* did not work. Finally the wind died just a little and I risked going broadside. The dock wasn't far — so we made it. This all lasted about a half hour, the longest half hour of my life. Now I never go out on a boat without the proper lifesaving equipment. I had taken a foolish, unnecessary risk, putting my son and myself way out on a limb.

"Not only did this scare me, but more importantly, it underlined my ongoing fear, my fear of water. Like most people, I can take momentary terror, probably because I'm too dim to realize the danger until it's over." He laughed. "Ongoing fear is something else, isn't it? It gnaws at you. I suspect my understanding of that gnawing fear accounts for my sailing across the Pacific Ocean with my son when he was nineteen. Part of a crew of six, we sailed three thousand three hundred miles in twenty-two days, out of the shipping lanes, with me as navigator and captain. The only professional aboard was our cook. To face my fear, I had to conquer the biggest chunk of water this planet has."

"Was it terrifying?"

He laughed.

"On the contrary," he said. "Wonderfully, that voyage held some of the happiest days of my life. It was well worth the risk."

"Besides swimming," I asked, "what else did you want to conquer when you were a child?"

"I remember something I wanted terribly to do," he said. "A neighbor boy had a pony, and I wanted to ride this pony in the worst way. I was terrified of the animal, though. Now you would think that my fear would cancel out my desire to ride the horse, but it didn't. I *had* to ride that pony!"

"What happened?"

"To start, I made a tactical blunder. Horses are wonderful creatures, and they can sense when you're in control. I had had a bicycle when I was eleven, a cheap, rusty two-wheeler without a chain guard. My pants leg always seemed to get caught in the chain, so I took to rolling up my pants leg. Now, picture this — here I am, about to mount this pony, and I'm rolling my pants leg up. The pony saw me do this and immediately must have thought I was an idiot. From that moment, *he* was the master of the situation. I did get on him, though, and I was thrilled to stay on. In some way, perhaps, a seed was planted there, because to this day I love to ride horses. I guess my point is, Walter, that it's not enough to take risks; we have to learn from them."

"Hugh," I asked, "*can* we learn to take risks?"

"Absolutely," he said. "If we start by taking small risks, we're encouraged to take larger risks — and if we know clearly what's at stake, we can take risks more wisely. For example, if I was asked whether I'd drive a car at a hundred and twenty-five miles per hour on Route 101, I'd have to reply yes and no! Just to drive it, I'd say no. The risk's too great. However, if I was told that my child was down the highway, in serious trouble, urgently needing my help, I'd say yes. And of course, to give ourselves the best chance for success with any risk, we must prepare well. Because I am a coward."

"A coward?"

"Indeed, a *devout* coward. I've always been that way about aviation, for example. I really stack the cards in my favor. Some people laugh when I go through a checklist, it's so thorough. I have no death wish. I check *everything*. I've seen pilots come to grief because they skipped the details. Good preparation reduces anxiety — and odds."

"Why do you take risks?"

"Walter," he replied, "no one matures without taking risks. We *must* take risks. In my own case, apparently, as I grew out of adolescence I created a momentum that's still going. My wife, in fact, suggests that my risk-taking is delayed adolescence. In a sense that may be true. Like a teenager, I'm eager to try new things. The difference is, though, I try not to take risks foolishly, and I really do try to follow my own advice, which means I must learn from the risks I take, I must know what's at stake, and I must prepare as if my life depends on it — because after all, it does."

"Do we mature all our lives?"

"I believe we should. It's like chess. You can learn chess in fifteen minutes, then spend the rest of your life trying to perfect your game. Let me see if I can give you an example. Yes! I remember one time I hit my hand with a hammer and cursed profanely.

"My son asked, 'Daddy, why don't you cry?'

"I said, 'I don't know. I'm into swearing.'

"He said, 'Daddies never cry.'

"I argued, 'But they do!' I began thinking that one measure of our maturity is what brings us to tears. If we cry because we are sorry for ourselves, that's less mature than crying because someone we love is in trouble. It's priorities, really."

"Hugh, how have you learned to establish priorities?"

"By answering to myself what's really important. Once, for example, when we lived in Wilmette, our home was robbed, some sentimental pieces were taken, but of particular significance was a watch that had belonged to my wife's father. Everything else, I concluded, was junk. Finally, I couldn't feel bitter, because I realized that if I had been a billionaire — had four billion dollars! — and someone evil had taken my child, how much I would pay to get him back."

"Four billion?" I suggested.

"All of it, of course. What's important in our lives is really important; the rest is junk."

"What's the worst risk we can take?" I asked.

"Not to choose," he replied. "To sit it out, ironically, is the worst risk of all. We should never leave our decisions to fate. When we don't choose, when we don't risk, we step out of the game. 'I should not have done that!' is easier to say than 'I wish I had tried.' Do you agree?"

"Yes," I said.

*

Hugh discovered, as have Liz Smith and so many other successful risk-takers, that we must look beyond ourselves to grow — but he also learned that risks begin, and are overcome, from within: "I stood on that beach while those waves crashed at my feet. I couldn't turn my back on it; I had to face my fear."

Let's visualize another risk. Imagine standing on one side of a rising drawbridge. If we hurry, we can leap across the widening gap, but a friend slows us, warning, "Look how far you could fall."

"But if we don't cross this bridge," we say, "we're stuck here — and this is not where we want to be."

"Maybe you should wait," our friend suggests, "until it's safer."

"But if we don't go *now*," we explain, "we'll miss out."

"Look!" squeals our friend, gesturing frantically at the opening, now even larger.

"We're wasting time," we tell each other. "C'mon, it's easy."

Is it?

The answer is not in the bridge; the answer is within us. The bridge can neither inspire us to leap nor prevent us from trying. Only we can decide. How badly do we want to reach the other side? Why?

Keep this picture in mind as a very confused adolescent — me — unwittingly steps to the edge.

I had to know what Rosemary felt about me. So at my urging, a friend of mine told her, "Walter likes you."

"He's nice," she said.

"Do you like him?" he pressed.

"I don't know," she replied.

"Well," my friend reported back to me, "she didn't say she didn't!"

"I don't care," I lied.

Both Rosemary and I were sixteen — thankfully, I was some months older — and she was popular in high school and, to my mind, quite beautiful. I, in contrast, felt like a toad. I hated my eyeglasses, could never seem to comb my hair right, knew with precision the location of every pimple on my forehead, and was a disappointing student, to say the least, at A. B. Davis High School in Mount Vernon, where I was failing or doing poorly in everything but English and gym.

"Walter," I'd heard often, "you can do better."

"I'll try," I'd promise.

Inside, I smoldered with self-doubt, wondering, who am I? *What am I going to do?* Thus, when I mustered the courage to speak with Rosemary myself, I tried to hide my insecurity behind a swagger, as if somehow a rejection from her would mean little to me.

"You don't want to go out, do you?"

"What?"

"Go out," I said. "Do you want to?"

"Where?"

She didn't say no, I realized. But now what? *Where?* What a jerk I am. What do I say?

"The movies," I replied.

"When?"

"Huh?"

"When?" she repeated.

"Uh . . ." I studied my feet. "Saturday?"

"What time?"

"Six o'clock?"

"I don't know." She hesitated.

That's that, I told myself. She's turning me down. My face reddened.

"Could we make it six-thirty?" she asked, explaining quickly, "I'll be finished with dinner by then."

"Yeah," I said, "that'll be okay."

For two nights I had trouble sleeping; I daydreamed during morning *and* afternoon classes. A small balloon seemed to swell in my stomach whenever I thought of Rosemary. Maybe, I hoped, she liked me.

Saturday night I grunted my way through saying hello to her parents.

"How are you?"

"Uh-huh." I smiled.

"How are you doing in school?"

"Uh-huh." Another smile.

"Do you like Davis High School?"

"Uh-uh." I frowned.

"Why not?"

I shrugged, paused, then, with some effort, spoke almost a sentence: "Just don't like school, I guess."

Somehow, despite my tongue-tied replies, Rosemary and I made it through the front door and into my car, a 1955 blue Packard Clipper Custom that had been my father's.

"Your parents are nice," I said. *Dumb*, I thought, what a dumb thing to say.

"Thank you," she told me, laughing. "I kind of like them."

Maybe it wasn't so dumb after all. "Yeah," I said, "they're *really* nice."

She laughed again.

My brain cells emptied; I had no thoughts. I could *feel* the silence in the car. Say something, I told myself. I felt the balloon swell inside my stomach. Say *something*.

"I'm going to be a Marine!" I declared.

"You *are*?"

Was that respect I heard in her voice?

"I think," she said, "they have the best uniforms!"

It *was* respect.

"I'll get my uniform right away," I told her, without the slightest clue as to whether or not that was true.

"Oh, I'd like to see you in it."

"Okay," I said, "as soon as I come home from boot camp."

"When will that be?"

"I don't know yet."

"When will you know?"

My older brother, Bill, who was married and lived several blocks away, had quietly been encouraging me to enlist in the service, as he himself had done about a decade earlier. I was confused, though, because as distressing as my life at home and on the street could be, it was still familiar to me. *It was what I knew*; military service was the dark unknown. Nevertheless, despite my trepidation, joining the Marines had crossed my mind several times since Slim had enlisted a year earlier. Even Tony's wild claim struck a chord inside me: "They're the baddest, and everybody respects 'em!" Tony, though, muscles and all, was turned down by the Marines, and he never told anyone why. Now my declaration to Rosemary was causing me to face up to what I really feared: Would the Marines reject *me*?

Rosemary and I had fun that night, chattering about the movie, not the Marines, on the way home. Then, after an awkward but pleasant moment at her door, I announced, "I'm going to talk to the recruiter in New Rochelle Monday after school."

I don't think I saw Rosemary again — because I did keep my word. Monday afternoon I saw the recruiter.

He said yes.

How tempting it would be to write here "And then I became a man." It would not be true, though. Enlisting in the Marine Corps was a step toward maturity, a move *within* adolescence.

Yes, within.

Picture three large steps. The first is childhood. Next up is adolescence. The highest is our adult years. Now let's look a little more closely at what we've constructed. The first step is actually a series of countless little steps. We grow from our first cell; we become less helpless with each passing day. A newborn is considerably different from a Terrible Two; a three-year-old is certainly not a nine-year-old. It's easy to marvel at how our bodies evolve. Even more impressive, though, is what happens unseen within our brains. Social scientists have discovered that somewhere between the ages of two and four we start to know right from wrong, and later, roughly between eight and ten, we begin to understand the concept of justice.

Adolescence, like childhood, is made up of steps within a step — and as I've said, this tumultuous stage of our lives generally does not end in our teens, as is popularly believed, or for that matter even in our early twenties.

I realize it would be foolish, impossible, to try to assign precise dates for change in human lives. Roughly drawn, though, there are three phases, or tiers, to the approximately *twenty*-year period we know as adolescence:

Phase One — From about ten or twelve to about seventeen or eighteen. Our struggle for identity begins in earnest: *Who am I?* We're self-absorbed; it's our most volatile time. The triangle is classic, observable through the centuries and in a thousand cultures: us, our parents, our friends. Emotionally, we try to separate ourselves from our parents while at the same time we're irresistibly drawn to our peers for approval. Although we often shout for nonconformity, rarely are we again so conforming. On one hand we reject the adult world, but on the other we adopt language, clothes, and style so similar to those of our friends that we look like we've all been stamped from a giant cookie cutter. We live for the present, for the moment; we fantasize a future of great success with minimal effort: I'm going to be rich! I'm going to be famous!

Phase Two — From about eighteen or nineteen to our early twenties. The future has become a concern. We're worried; we can no longer shut out the adult world. We ask ourselves, what am I going to do? I must do *something*. But what? *Who am I?* We test ourselves, often by leaving home. Our career plans change, our expectations sometimes become lower, and our risks start to focus more on self-support. We grow more confident as we successfully face challenges on our own. Because the dramatic physical changes of puberty are over, we're more comfortable with our bodies than we were earlier. In our first phase we were up on a hill overlooking the ocean. Now we're standing on the sandy beach, occasionally sticking our toes in the water.

Phase Three — From the middle to late twenties. We have a better idea of what our lives will be. We seem to be swimming out into the sea, testing our strength and limits — but, still self-absorbed, we're not as confident as we appear. We look like adults. We may even be married, have children, appear quite successful, but subtle and substantial adjustments to the adult world continue. As we struggle, inexorably drawn to adulthood, our insecurity flares and we challenge relationships at home and at the workplace. We are still asking, *who am I?*

Few people I've known have answered the question as well as the woman we're about to meet.

Her large brown eyes were joyous, electric, and she smiled widely as she stepped off the elevator two minutes early for our luncheon date at the Polo Lounge of the Beverly Hills Hotel. Her pale blond hair, swept high and away, was elegantly styled, and her complexion was smooth, soft, and pink, her face as delicate and graceful as the star herself. Only a few hours earlier she had received a Golden Globe Award for her performance as the dowager empress in the television miniseries *Anastasia: The Mystery of Anna*, and on this day, February 1, 1987, she had another reason to celebrate, if she chose to. This was the forty-second anniversary, perhaps to the hour, of the morning that she learned she had finally won one of the most significant lawsuits in the history of Hollywood — a victory that not only freed her and thousands of others from unfair contract clauses, but also changed forever the relationship between actors and movie studios. Since that courtroom triumph, she had earned two Oscars, another Golden Globe, scores of other honors. She had been the lonely spinster in *To Each His Own*, the shy, homely Catherine Sloper in *The Heiress*, and, of course, Melanie in *Gone With the Wind* — and it was she, Olivia de Havilland, one of the most respected actresses of all time, who had dared to risk it all by challenging the system. I intended to ask her about it.

"Walter!" she hailed me. "Oh my, I'm not late, am I?"

"No," I told her. "You're right on the button."

We had been together only a few seconds when a slender, neatly dressed older woman tentatively, shyly approached us at the entrance to the Polo Lounge.

"I must thank you, Miss de Havilland," she said, her voice rising, "for all the joy you've given us over the years."

"Thank *you*," Olivia replied, grasping her hands.

The woman beamed.

A few minutes later, as we shared a quiet corner booth, I considered the extraordinary dignity of my luncheon companion. She wore a tailored, purple, knee-length silk dress closed at the neck with a matching bow. Her earrings were gold and pearl — simple, elegant. Here, I knew, was a woman who had left home at sixteen and later shaken the very pillars of an industry. Yet here too, I would learn, was a woman who had stood humiliated as a teenager before her classmates, a woman who doubted, despite her spectacular success, that she had found her destiny, whose one real regret was a risk she hadn't taken.

"Olivia," I said, "I'd like to see if this rings a bell with you." Her eyebrows raised and her concentration focused.

Slowly I read aloud:

> "I'd like to be a pirate bold,
> And steal some silver and some gold.
> I'd plunder every single sea
> And make the people scared of me.
> I'd be in every history book
> Because of all the ships I took."

Olivia de Havilland had written the poem six decades earlier, when she was ten years old, and titled it "Pirates."

"Now what do you suppose this means?" I asked.

"Well," she started, a light chuckle in her voice, "there must be a meaning I intended. Hearing you read it now, I see a desire for fame. 'I'd be in every history book because of all the ships I took.' Do you see that in there?"

"I think so," I said. "Where did you live when you wrote the poem?"

"In Saratoga, California, a beautiful village in the Santa Clara Valley — now called Silicon Valley. When I was a child, it was filled with prune orchards, and in the spring it was a sea of white blossoms, a glorious sight. It was there I dreamed of being a pirate, there at the base of the Santa Cruz range, just over the mountains from the ocean."

There, I remembered her telling me during a breakfast we had shared together a few months earlier in Manhattan, was a place for a girl to dream marvelous adventures, to laugh, to skip among flowers, to titter with classmates — but *there*, I knew, was also a place of pain.

"Olivia," I asked, "would you tell me again about speaking before a class at Los Gatos Union High School?"

"I suffer trauma to this day over that," she said. "I must have been seventeen at the time. Two years before, when I was a sophomore, I had been elected secretary of the student body, which, as you can imagine, was a very high honor. Thus I had, I thought, wonderful relations with my classmates. Well, in my senior year I was assigned the job of campaign manager for a girl who was running for president of the school, and as part of this large responsibility, I was to speak before each class for a minute or two. The first room I entered was a civics class. Very seriously, I described my candidate's qualifications and her platform. They *booed* me! I was humiliated, dejected. Worse, instead of crying, I reacted with hostility — the most foolish thing I could have done, in a sense booing back out of hurt. I feel the humiliation even now, thinking about it. I made the damage far worse by reacting to their rudeness. In a sense, I guess I helped validate their bad behavior. I fled that room in disgrace, *not* because my fellow students rejected me, *not* because of their hooting and heckling, but more because of my own angry, silly response."

"How would you respond today?"

"That's a good question — and I've had a lifetime to think about it. I'd take a risk. I'd try my hardest to be humorous, to be affectionate — which is precisely how I should have acted then."

"Last night," I reminded her, "you sat quietly as the Golden Globe nominees were named. Then they announced that you were the winner, and even though you've received two Academy Awards, an earlier Golden Globe, countless other citations and honors, worldwide critical acclaim, this award was important, wasn't it?"

"Yes, it was — and I was astonished. When they opened the envelope, it was an extraordinary feeling, like a paralysis. I had not expected to win. What had been going through my mind was, 'Olivia, be a good sport.' Because all of us like to see disappointments taken good-naturedly. Smile, I told myself, and remember to applaud enthusiastically for the winner. I had no thought of winning. When they called my name, I thought, 'There must be some mistake.' Then at the podium I checked, and I saw my name on the card and I knew I had won a Golden Globe, thirty-seven years after my first. Wonderful! When I left the stage, though, I left with two things in hand, the Golden Globe and the card with my name on it."

"What do you think that teenager who fell apart would have thought of the way you accepted your award?"

"She would be *very* pleased."

We both laughed.

"Olivia," I asked, serious again, "why did that teenager leave home?"

"You have to understand," she began, "that my parents had been divorced and we lived with my stepfather, who was very strict. Lights had to be out at eight-fifteen, even if we had not finished our homework. I remember once writing a history thesis by the light of a flashlight under my blankets. Fortunately, no matter how unreasonable my stepfather might be, I loved my studies. I'm sure most parents encourage their children to achieve A's. It was perplexing that although my stepfather would have been disappointed if I had not been an A student, instead of being supportive, he made it very difficult. Another rule he insisted on was no extracurricular activities. *None.* He ordered me home on the three-twenty bus, no exceptions. Now this posed an even greater problem than the lights-out. Without financial assistance, I couldn't afford to attend college when I graduated from high school, but to win a scholarship, in addition to high grades, I had to demonstrate an interest in school activities. Thus I was trapped."

"How badly did you want to attend college?"

"Very badly."

"What did you do?"

"When I was sixteen, I auditioned for a school play, and fortunately I was chosen for a leading role. This was a good extracurricular activity for me, because I could handle the day-time rehearsals, and my stepfather didn't arrive home until after six o'clock."

"It didn't work, though, did it?"

"No, it surely didn't."

"How did he find out?"

"My mother had to inform him of my plans one night be-cause at the last minute I had to attend a dress rehearsal. The next morning at breakfast my mother reported his orders to me:

" 'Your stepfather says you either withdraw from the play or you leave this house.'

"That was my choice. Quit or leave."

"You left?"

"Yes," she said, softly, "and I never returned."

"At sixteen, Olivia, could you understand the risk you were taking?"

"I saw no choice. I had given my word to perform. The tickets had been sold. That first night away from home I stayed with friends. Then I tried to find a place. After school on the following day, I interviewed with a woman who told me I could stay with her, do her laundry and ironing. I remember that after I left her, I realized that I had stayed too long, that I had missed all of the buses back to my friend's house. Alone, I started to walk. Four miles. Never have I been so depressed. It was a depression I can't forget. It had a color to it, a deep purple. Utter despair."

She paused, her last words trailing.

"Then?"

"To my surprise, when I arrived at my friend's, I found a message from my mother. She and her friends had collected two hundred dollars to see me through the rest of my junior year. They had also found a little bedroom for me in the house of a retired woman. The following summer, when I turned seventeen, I supported myself as a kitchen helper and as a cleaning girl for two families on vacation. Earlier I had given my mother a letter for my father, not my stepfather, and she saw to it that he received it in San Francisco, where he had come from Japan for a short business visit. When he learned what had happened, he decided to send me fifty dollars a month, which supported me through my senior year. In May I passed an entrance exam to Stanford University, an achievement that was relayed to Mills College. My success with the Stanford test, my high school grades, and my extracurricular activities, my acting — all together, I was awarded a scholarship to Mills College!"

"How did you feel?"

"Absolutely thrilled. Joyous! I was so glad I had taken the risk."

"Was it worth the deep purple despair?"

"Even *that!*"

She clapped her hands, laughing.

"Mills College was not to be, though, was it?"

"No, it was not. That summer, after I appeared in a local amateur production of *A Midsummer Night's Dream*, I read in the San Francisco *Chronicle* that the great director Professor Max Reinhardt had been invited to direct the same play in the Hollywood Bowl, in the San Francisco Opera House, and at the University of California."

"So you asked a friend at the California Festival Association if you could attend the rehearsals as an observer?"

"Yes. I was introduced to an assistant to Max Reinhardt, who suggested that since I was there anyway, I should try some lines. I read Puck, leaping over chairs — all very animated. The next day I was told to meet the company in Hollywood, that I would understudy the role of Hermia."

"Were you stunned?"

"Absolutely! This was unimaginable! I was assigned to be a second understudy, but shortly the first understudy left to appear in a movie. Gloria Stewart, who was to play Hermia, was already filming in another movie, leaving me to rehearse her role. Five nights before opening, Professor Reinhardt told me that Gloria Stewart was not returning. 'You will play Hermia,' he said. I agonized: What should I do? I didn't want to lose my scholarship, but this was a great opportunity, and more importantly, I knew I couldn't let the professor and the rest of the company down. I got in touch with Mills. They agreed to hold the scholarship open for me until February."

"Describe opening night."

"Terror. I was so frightened, I had to hide behind a bush to throw up. I mean, really throw up, in the most extreme way.

"Then someone announced, 'You're on.'

"I froze.

"I was pushed on stage. I remember staring, numb, at my fellow actor John Lodge, who later became the ambassador to Spain. In total paralysis I watched his mouth move, not hearing his words. I thought, 'He's supposed to cue me.' Then his mouth stopped. I started to talk. Words came out, words that were totally incomprehensible to me. John didn't seem surprised. They were apparently the right words. We left the stage — and the audience applauded! I couldn't believe it. It was a little like last night. I felt paralyzed, numb to the applause, but as we stepped off the stage, suddenly I felt a wave of exhilaration — and I couldn't wait to get back on."

"And you never went to Mills?"

"No," she said, taking a long breath, exhaling slowly, pausing.

"Walter," she started again, "I was weak. Reinhardt wanted two of the stage players, Mickey Rooney and me, to appear in the movie of *A Midsummer Night's Dream*, which was scheduled for filming in February. If I accepted, there was a possibility that Mills College might still hold the scholarship open, at least until September. This was very important to me, because I did not want to be a movie actress."

"You didn't? Why not?"

"In those days there was great snobbery about the theater — misplaced, but pervasive. Not only in the popular view, but in the art itself, theater was considered infinitely superior to cinema. Mills College was ideal preparation for *theater*."

"What happened?"

"The studio, Warner Brothers, insisted that I sign a three-month contract, which was fine, except they added a clause that at the end of that period, they could, if they chose, hold me to a seven-year contract.

" 'No,' I said, 'I can't do that. I'm going to college.'

"The people at Warner Brothers told me that either I signed with the seven-year option or I would be out of the movie.

" 'Then I guess I'm out,' I said.

"As I was leaving the studio, I ran into Professor Reinhardt, his assistant, and his producer. I thanked them but explained why I couldn't participate, that I was determined to attend Mills College, that Warner Brothers insisted I sign what was really a seven-year commitment. They became very excited — speaking in German — and literally propelled me into a casting room.

" 'We agree!' they assured me.

" 'You do?' I asked, surprised.

" 'Yes,' they said, 'seven years is too long. We'll have them make it *five* years.'

" 'Oh, if you can reduce it to five years . . .' I assured them that I'd play Hermia — and I regret it to this day."

"But isn't that what you wanted?"

"No, it was not — but unsure, anxious, eager to please, I allowed myself to be swayed. Truly, five years was as damaging, as far as my prospects for higher education were concerned, as seven. Mills College was the risk I should have taken. Today, looking back, I realize that if I had stuck to my guns, Warner Brothers probably would have agreed to a different clause, one that guaranteed I sign with them if I decided after graduation to pursue a career in movies. Such an option surely would have protected the studio, and it would have allowed me both to appear in *A Midsummer Night's Dream* and to attend college."

"Ironically," I said, "had Warner done just that, the studio may have lost less in the long run."

"That's true," she said, nodding, "but no one could have known that at the time."

"Following *A Midsummer Night's Dream*," I reminded Olivia, "you were Joe E. Brown's leading lady in *Alibi Ike* and James Cagney's co-star in *The Irish in Us*, and you completed your first of nine films with Errol Flynn, *Captain Blood*."

She nodded.

"And eventually you agreed to a seven-year contract."

She nodded again.

"And during this time the studios had a practice of lending actors to each other, at a profit — often at a price higher than what the actor was paid."

"That's true."

"And the roles assigned to you by Warner Brothers began to be . . . well, tedious."

"Yes," she said, laughing, "that's *certainly* true. Time and again I was cast as a romantic heroine, a one-dimensional character. In the beginning it was fun. I loved *Captain Blood* and *Robin Hood*, but I longed for something more difficult, more challenging. I studied the performances of other actresses, wonderful, talented people like Bette Davis. I wanted to do the kind of work Bette was doing right on our own lot."

"You became depressed?"

"Yes, seriously depressed. Then came the role of Melanie in *Gone With the Wind*. This too would be a loan-out — MGM would distribute it for David Selznick."

"What happened?"

"Jack Warner said no."

"Why?"

"He told me, 'It's going to be the biggest bust in years. Not only that, if I let you go, you'll be difficult when you come back.'

" 'I won't be difficult,' I promised.

" 'No,' he said.

" 'Please,' I pleaded.

" 'No,' he told me. So I did something pretty bold. I invited Jack Warner's wife — she had been an actress herself, Ann Alvarado — to tea at the Brown Derby in Beverly Hills. I explained to her how important this role was to me, how important acting was to me. 'I understand,' she told me. 'I'll see what I can do to persuade Jack.' And she succeeded!"

"He warmed to the idea?"

"Not exactly. In exchange for me, he negotiated a one-picture deal with Jimmy Stewart. Jack was, if anything, a businessman."

"Were you difficult when you returned?"

"Not at first. After all, I had given my word."

"How were you treated?"

"Poorly. The first picture Jack assigned me when I returned

was *Elizabeth and Essex*, with Errol Flynn. Jack demoted me. In our previous movies, Errol and I had been co-stars, but in *Elizabeth and Essex* I was to be a lady-in-waiting. Bette Davis was the co-star. Also, my billing was dropped. My name was printed smaller and placed beneath the title."

"What did you do?"

"I had given my word. I went along with it."

"It hurt?"

"It hurt."

"What was the next picture?"

"A remake of *Saturday's Children*, which I knew had to flop. The original had been with Corinne Griffith and Grant Withers. Career-wise, I knew *Saturday's Children* was a mistake for me. It had to fail. So I declined."

"You received your first suspension?"

"Yes."

"What happened when *Gone With the Wind* was scheduled for release?"

"It was to open in Atlanta, and Jack, at that very moment, cast me in something called *Flight Number Eight*. I read the script and realized this plane would never get off the ground. Jack was being retributive. *Flight Number Eight* had to be another flop, because the original, with Ronald Colman and Kay Francis, had been done with great style. I'd had enough."

"Did he suspend you again?"

"Yes — and the catch was that the period of each suspension was automatically added to the end of my contract, which was studio practice at the time. Jack also forbade me to attend the opening of *Gone With the Wind*."

"*Gone With the Wind* became a spectacular success, though, and you were nominated for an Academy Award. And you continued to act in movies for Jack Warner?"

"Yes. Then my contract ended, in May 1943. I had started

to serve my suspension time when Jack loaned me out to Columbia for a picture at four times my salary —"

"With *him*," I interrupted, "keeping the money?"

"Of course," she said laughing. "And this film had barely twenty pages of script. The movie hadn't even been written! Doomed, I thought. Another flop in the making. What do I do? My agent told me that an attorney had advised him of a California law that limited an employee contract to seven years — a fact that could mean that the practice of tacking suspension time onto contracts was invalid. 'But,' he warned me, 'no actor has dared challenge the studio system.'

" 'I want to read the law myself,' I told him.

"I did, and to me, the intent was clear. The practice *was* wrong. So I asked the attorney, 'What do I do?'

" 'There are three steps,' the attorney explained. 'First comes the California Superior Court, in which Warner's lawyers will grill you on the witness stand to make you look like a spoiled, temperamental brat. They'll provoke you, trick you — whatever's necessary. Next is the appellate court, in which a three-judge panel will rule on the superior court's decision. Then the third recourse, if we need it, is the Supreme Court.'

" 'All right,' I told him. 'Let's do it. But let's not stop. We see this through to the end, no matter what.' "

"Olivia," I said, "*no matter what* could have ended your career, couldn't it?"

"Yes."

"You had been a star for nine years, had been praised for your role as Melanie, had earned a good income — how did you assess the risk?"

"If I lost, I'd be directed to serve the extension time, and undoubtedly Jack would make me an example and make me miserable, I'm sure, with the worst possible roles. Simply, he would wreck my career. Also, because my contract was for

personal services, if I lost I'd be prohibited from working elsewhere. On the other hand, what I had to lose by not fighting
was just as bad — and that would be to give in and do films
I knew in my heart could not work."

"How were you treated in the courtroom?"

"Exactly as the attorney had warned. Warner's lawyers tried
every tactic to provoke me:

" 'Is it not true that on such-and-such a date you deliberately
and willfully refused to report for work?'

" 'I declined,' I'd say.

"The lawyer became rude, belligerent in tone, provoking —
but I held my temper.

"Let me say this, Walter. Inside, I wanted to throttle that
man. He was so nasty. But I held fast. Outside the court, the
pressure grew even greater. Stories and pictures started to appear in the newspapers in which Warner advertised — all por-
traying me as spoiled and fractious. I had left for a USO hospital tour in the Aleutians, where, in Adak, I received a
telegram:

" 'You won,' it read.

"Warner immediately appealed and enjoined one hundred
and fifty movie companies from hiring me. In the appellate
court, it seemed from the questioning that one of the judges
leaned toward Warner's view, but the ruling was unanimous
in my favor. Warner again enjoined movie companies from
hiring me. He even enjoined companies that were out of business!"

"When did you win?"

"Forty-two years ago today, when the Supreme Court ruled
the decisions of the lower courts valid. I was free! I never made
another movie for Warner."

"And within a year you were nominated and received an
Academy Award for *To Each His Own*?"

"Yes."

"How did you feel about the impact your case had on the movie industry?"

"Truly, that was thrilling. Men like Clark Gable and Jimmy Stewart had taken real risks as servicemen during the war, while their contracts were being extended by the studios. Because of the decision in my case, they were able to renegotiate when they returned home. It was Jimmy, in fact, who asked a court to rule on how my case affected the contracts of veterans. I felt very good about that."

"What have you learned from your experiences about taking risks?"

"Many of the decisions you face in your life have to do with feeling comfortable with yourself. Some, if you think them through honestly, are not as difficult as they might seem. Despite the problems, for example, it was easier for me to leave my stepfather's house than to stay there."

"Do you regret any risks?"

"Only those I didn't take. One in particular — I regret not having the courage to say no to Professor Reinhardt early on, when I was first offered a contract. Please don't misunderstand. My life has had great rewards, but still, deep inside, I have the conviction I had another destiny — and somehow it involved going to Mills College. I regret my weakness."

"Olivia," I asked, "what do you suppose that destiny might have been?"

"I'm sure it would have involved people, perhaps teaching or working in the social sciences. Actors have talents, like sensitivity, that are valuable in other fields. I'll never know, because I did not take the risk. Also, in a different path I may have found the one man with whom I could have spent my whole life — something that was important to me, something that has not been fulfilled. That, of course, is the problem when we avoid a risk. We never know, do we? That's worse than failure."

"Do you fear failure?"

"I did fear failure, almost pathologically, but I do not any longer."

"Why?"

"Finally, Walter, I've learned from experience. We should not seek to fail, but now I understand that sometimes something marvelous can occur only if you go through that doorway. Success can be the child of disappointment."

"Like your trouble at Warner's — and the subsequent Academy Awards and even greater screen success?"

"Yes."

"Where do you find the strength?"

"It's there in each of us, if we call on it. We must take risks. True self-confidence comes from practice. We must *do!*"

Olivia's insight — "We must *do!*" — is vivid to me as I recall a night in what I now understand as the beginning of the second phase of my adolescence.

Traces of moonlight flickered across the silent, orderly rows of dark green blankets, each one wrapped around a sleeping body. I studied one slight, moving beam, a single mesmerizing shaft of light, and watched it scatter faintly across a wall — no, a bulkhead. I followed it to the ceiling — no, the overhead. Enough, I thought. Why can't I sleep?

I was seventeen, a Marine private first class stationed at Camp Lejeune, North Carolina.

Again I studied my watch: 0200.

Why can't I sleep? What's troubling me? Hidden behind the thickening clouds that crowded my mind was an idea, maybe a problem — and I couldn't reach it, couldn't quite touch it.

Resigned to a sleepless night, I slid quietly out of my rack, slipped on my green utility trousers and my green utility jacket, laced my black boots, donned my green hat (my cover), stepped through the door (the hatch), and lit a Pall Mall.

I had enlisted only seven months earlier, in September 1961, but I felt like I had been in the Marine Corps all my life. Did I dream the rest?

I wondered, do I have a home somewhere? Am I ever getting out? That's it! Am I ever getting out?

During the past few weeks, two short-timers in my outfit had been released, having completed their four-year enlistments. Prior to their discharge, not a day went by without the banter:

"How short are you?"

"I'm so short, I got to look up to look down."

"Can someone help me with my socks?"

"Why?"

"I'm too short. Can't reach 'em."

I, on the other hand, was a new Marine, a boot, so I was teased:

"Anderson, tell me again, how long you got?"

"Three years and five months."

"Three years! And what? I don't even have time to say it! I'm too short . . ."

It could just as easily have been three *hundred* years; for me, it was eternity. And I was confused. When I had gone home on leave three months before, after about a hundred days of boot camp at Parris Island in South Carolina and advanced infantry training at Camp Lejeune, I had noticed quickly how different I found my home.

I saw litter outside. Along Third Street I eyeballed cigarette butts, patches of lint and dirt, candy wrappers, beer cans strewn about the deck — I mean, the street. An hour earlier, riding the subway from Manhattan to 241st Street, I had remained standing, not wanting to crease or soil my trousers.

I saw colors. Having lived from dawn to dark surrounded,

immersed, in Marine green during my first few months of training, I found that the streets of Mount Vernon and its lights, the parked cars, the disordered rows of houses and office buildings, the billboards, the clothes the civilians wore all made a spectacular rainbow.

Where do I belong? There, I wondered, or here? Will I ever get out?

That's *not* it.

Involuntarily, I breathed deeply. It was coming to me. I crushed my cigarette, then field-stripped the tobacco and paper.

I *will* get out.

The words flashed like neon, bursting a dam, flooding me with unbalanced, conflicting thoughts.

What will I do? *Nothing.*

I'm a kid. *No, I'm not.*

I'm a Marine. *I'm still a kid.* No, I'm not. *Yes, I am.*

Shaken, I returned to my rack, undressed silently, crawled under the blanket, and lay my head on the pillow, my eyes wide.

I have to be a man. There's no escape; I can't be a kid anymore. *I have to be a man.* In three years and five months (suddenly it didn't seem so long!) I'll be a civilian, on my own. I'll be twenty-one. I'll be a man.

Twenty-one? It seemed old.

No one knew I cried that night. My agony, fueled by self-doubt, was as painful as any I've experienced. Looking through the long lens of twenty-six years, I know now that in that darkness, amid the shadows flickering across the still racks, I took my first step on what would have to be a long march out of adolescence.

A few hours later, in daylight, I asked to see the first sergeant.

"What's up?" he asked.

"I want to go to school," I said.

*

Although I was still an adolescent as I weighed my future, the maturity of my decision this time — to go to school — was greater, more insightful, than the choice I had made to enlist. I had joined the Marines to impress my peers, to *belong*; it was a blind risk. Now, alone with my thoughts, I had finally begun to grasp what was at stake.

My awakening in the dark of the night at Camp Lejeune reminds me of an answer I received one afternoon when I asked W. Clement Stone, the irrepressible eighty-six-year-old millionaire philanthropist, whether people can learn to take risks. He replied, "Yes, but they *must* have a goal."

Clement, who has given away a quarter of a billion dollars, was born without wealth in Chicago. I knew he had been raised by his mother, a dressmaker, and had started his own insurance company (one of several he would create) with a hundred dollars when he was twenty.

"What if you had failed?" I asked.

"Walter," he said, "I *have* failed. But what I've learned is that with every adversity there's an equivalent benefit for whoever will apply it. When I fail, I thank God for the opportunity the experience gives me. I learn from whatever mistakes I've made. Then I try again."

"Do you regret any risks you've taken?"

"No," he replied. "And it wouldn't matter to me whether a particular risk succeeded or not. I am sure of one thing, though."

"What's that?"

"If I had a regret, it would be for risks I *didn't* take."

Whether we're children learning to trust, teenagers striving to be accepted by our peers, as I was when I joined the Marines, or adults seeking respect in the workplace, like W. Clement Stone, our needs — and the risks they inspire — rarely diminish. Conversations among people of all ages bubble with "afters" and "if onlys": after this semester, after graduation, after the next promotion, after the baby's in school, after the kids get married, after we retire; if only we had a car or a better car, a house or a better house, smaller troubles, fewer bills, more savings.

And risks *escalate*.

How this happens can be seen particularly well in the career of a good friend who is a social scientist trusted by millions — Dr. Joyce Brothers.

It was a few weeks before Christmas 1986 when I interviewed Joyce, an honors graduate of Cornell who had earned a master's and a doctorate at Columbia and become one of America's most popular psychologists. Since 1955, when she first appeared as a contestant on *The $64,000 Question* quiz show, she has become a renowned newspaper and magazine columnist and a radio and television personality of considerable force. Audiences *like* her — and I know why. It's reflected in the books she writes, books such as *How to Get Whatever You Want Out of Life* and *What Every Woman Should Know About Men*, and it's in her voice. She *cares*.

Now, as she was seated in my office, I studied my guest. She was tiny — an inch over five feet tall and hardly a hundred pounds. She was in her late fifties; her hair was blond, natural, styled full and neat, and her eyes, behind large brown-framed glasses, were light blue. She wore a brown suede jacket with a matching skirt. A white-gold wedding band with baguettes was her only jewelry; her fingernails were clear and perfectly manicured.

Joyce Brothers, whom I have known for years, is a risk-taker whose self-control is legendary. One afternoon on her radio show a caller threatened suicide, and Joyce stayed cool and kept the woman calm, finally saving her life — but I knew that as collected as Joyce seemed to be that day, she was shaken by the ordeal. It was about this contrast — considering the *other* side of Dr. Brothers — that I sought to question my friend, and I hoped also that she'd be able to help me illustrate how risks escalate, which meant she would have to re-examine the way in which her own acclaim began.

"What prompted you to go on *The $64,000 Question*?" I asked.

"We could not make ends meet. My husband was a medical school graduate doing his residency. I was a young mother who also taught at Hunter College and Columbia University and did research work in psychology. Together we earned a little more than five thousand dollars a year. To get by, with money so tight, we had to live at home with my parents, and as much as we all loved each other, it was too hard for my folks not to tell us what to do. So, as you'd expect, there was tension under the roof. Then one night, while watching *The $64,000 Question* on television, I noticed that the losers received a new Cadillac after reaching a minimum level. How lucky they are, I told myself. We could live for several years on the price of that Cadillac. If I was awarded a car like that, I thought, we'd sell it right away. *If I received one!* I wondered, why not?"

"Is that when you began to study the show?"

"Yes," she replied, "and I discovered that the contestants chosen for the program almost always seemed to be an unlikely pairing with their subject. For example, a Marine Corps captain was a gourmet chef, a tiny gray-haired grandmother was a baseball expert, and a shoemaker was an opera buff. I was fascinated — and I was challenged. Thus, I decided to try to be a contestant — for two reasons. I thought it would be an exciting, interesting experience, and, as I've said, my husband and I had real need; I wanted that Cadillac to sell."

"Did you think you had much at risk?"

"Not in the beginning," she said. "My risk seemed small at first. At the very worst, I expected to lose quickly — and get the Cadillac."

"There were surprises, though, weren't there?"

"Yes," she said, laughing, "and some were good and some, as you know, were not so good."

"How did you get started?"

"Well, I knew I had to pick a topic that was not vast and inexhaustible; I had to avoid broad topics like English literature and world history. I knew I had to study something finite, an area of interest in which I could actually become expert — and even more important, it had to be a subject that was unlikely to be of interest to a rather small young female psychologist. I settled on two topics. One was boxing, the other plumbing. I chose boxing, because it was more exciting and, being less than a century old, it was a subject I could learn. If I can grasp quantum theory, I told myself, I can memorize boxing statistics and records. I knew a little about boxing, because my husband was a fan and we would watch it on television."

"How did you proceed?"

"I visited Nat Fleischer, who was the editor and the owner of *Ring* magazine. I told him precisely what I intended to do, and he loved the idea! 'Joyce,' he said, 'if you do well, it will be wonderful for boxing.' Then he made available every resource and record of boxing he had, including all issues of his magazine to that date. He showed me the best encyclopedias and books on the subject, and he directed me to Jimmy Jacobs, who owned the best film library of boxing in the world. And Jimmy loaned me his clips of the greatest fights of the century, which meant my husband and I had to make a large investment, forty dollars a month, to rent a projector to view Jimmy's films. Eight weeks later, after daily study, I had memorized the history of the heavyweight, light heavyweight, and middleweight divisions."

"The risks began to multiply, didn't they?"

"Yes. At this point we had eighty dollars invested in projector rental fees — and my time. I had stopped working in order to raise our daughter, so it didn't matter how I spent my evenings, whether I studied boxing or did something else. The eighty dollars, though, was a lot of money to us. I knew it was time to act. I wrote to the program and explained that I was a mother, a psychologist, and an expert on boxing. Then I waited.

"I remember I was contacted quickly — by telegram. We planned this well, I thought. The message said 'Call here immediately.' So I did.

" 'What are you doing right now?' a man at the number asked me.

" 'I just washed my hair.' I told him the truth.

" 'Come right down!' he said.

" 'My hair's wet.'

" 'Put a towel on your head,' he told me, 'and come down here right now.' I hesitated. 'We'll pay for the cab,' he added.

"I grabbed a towel and was on my way."

I started to laugh, a curious and amusing picture forming in my mind of my friend Dr. Joyce Brothers speeding into a cab with a bath-towel turban flapping in the breeze.

"What happened next?" I asked.

"They tested me at the studio by opening several books at random to find questions. I answered all correctly. 'You're accepted,' they told me. 'But you won't be on for a while. Use the time to study.'

"And I did. I'd start at six in the morning and continue until one the next morning, interrupting my study only to care for our daughter —"

"Joyce," I interrupted, "how did you perceive the size of the risk then?"

"It had changed," she replied. "I would no longer be satisfied with being a loser, receiving a Cadillac. Money, which had been my original reason to try to go on the show, became less important. My husband, I realized, was going to earn a good income once he was established, and when I was able to practice full-time again, we'd both do well. No, I admitted to myself, the consolation prize was no longer a satisfactory reward. Deep down I knew I wanted to have experiences and I wanted to be famous. Suddenly the risk was very large. *What if I fail? I'll be on national television. What if I embarrass myself?"*

"How did you weigh your risks?"

"Before I was accepted, all I could think about was the car. When I was told that I'd actually be a contestant, a window opened for me, one with larger opportunities and a new goal: *I'm going for the sixty-four-thousand-dollar question.* Once I realized — admitted to myself — my new objective, the risks really grew. Consciously, I thought about the up side and the down side. If I won on the show, I'd have success, certainly fame. I began to think of my life as a wall built with bricks. If I did well, a foundation brick would be set. I'd be known all over, admired, and my chances would be endless. But if I failed, I'd be acutely embarrassed. The show was immensely popular. The same spotlight that could make me famous could devastate me, I realized, if I performed poorly. If you remember, the format was a series of questions, each of which led, if you continued to answer correctly, to a more difficult and valuable question, and finally to the one worth sixty-four thousand dollars. If I won up to sixteen thousand dollars, let's say, then lost, no one would say Joyce Brothers won sixteen thousand; they'd say she *failed* at thirty-two thousand. I'd be seen as a loser, and the thought stung. First the money became less important; then it became not important at all. *Everything* changed for me."

"How nervous did you get?"

"Walter," she replied, her tone flat, "it took over my life. On the day of each show — remember, each contestant appeared week after week to create drama for the TV audience — I'd feel enormous pressure. The hours after the show and the following day would be pleasant. I'd be congratulated. I'd feel like a human being. I would be decent to my husband and to my friends. Then the next show would draw closer. It was as if I was in the middle of a progressive illness, as if I needed oxygen but couldn't reach it. The pressure inside me increased daily. What made it worse is that my husband and father, the two men I loved, fought bitterly — instead of easing tension, their bickering increased it. It was the worst time in my family life. More than once I considered quitting, just to stop their arguing. I was frightened. Again the risks multiplied. I worried: can I lose my family over this?"

"How did you respond?"

She drew a deep breath, exhaled slowly. "When I get that terrified," she replied, "I grow cold. I knew I couldn't control my family or the show. But I *could* control me. Fear makes me icy. I lose control only when I'm angry, not when I'm afraid —"

"And that presented another problem, didn't it?"

"Yes," she said. "Some of the people behind the show, like the late Charles Revson, actually hated me. In their eyes, I was not good theater. I looked totally controlled. I didn't sweat. How could they know — and they certainly did not care — what I was experiencing inside? Unfortunately, I made it look easy. Lousy drama."

"What *did* you feel inside?"

"Even talking about it now, I feel it, as if I have a high fever, as if I'm trembling with a shaking chill. But I don't show it on the outside. That's me."

"Was it later, when *The $64,000 Question* was investigated by a congressional committee, that you first found out that they had tried to make you a loser?"

"Yes, it was. I learned they tended to give easy questions to some contestants and very difficult ones to those whom they were trying to trip up. From their sponsor's testimony, it seemed my calm demeanor was not the drama they wanted. After my sixteen-thousand-dollar answer, every question was specifically designed for me to lose. To me it had seemed very simple up to the sixteen-thousand-dollar question. After that I just thought it was tough, as difficult as I had expected it to be."

"And after you gave the thirty-two-thousand-dollar answer, they asked you if you'd risk it all, go double or nothing, go for the sixty-four-thousand-dollar question. Why did you decide to take the risk?"

"It came to a simple choice. I could keep the thirty-two thousand dollars and leave the show a winner. The tension at home between my father and my husband would cease. I'd be a heroine and I would be famous as a winner. Or I could bet it all — and possibly fail, which meant the audience would remember me only as a loser, the psychologist who lost sixty-four thousand dollars. Because the money aspect had diminished in importance to me, I knew my biggest risk was not the money. I could lose that and still sleep well. My true risk was the terrible embarrassment I imagined I'd suffer in a public failure — thank goodness I didn't know the real odds stacked against me — so alone I asked myself, *can I take the loss?* Can I face the worst?"

"Why did you go ahead?"

"I did it for *me*. I had to confront the worst; I had to face my fear of embarrassment. Looking back, I understand now that I had triumphed long before I correctly answered the sixty-four-thousand-dollar question. The truth is, the right answer — winning the money — was anticlimactic and small compared to my real achievement, which was to make the decision to take the risk."

"Was that," I asked, "your *greatest* risk?"

"Yes," she replied.

"Did you cry?"

"No," she said.

"Why not?"

"I was just too worried; I had to control myself. When I feel fear that intensely, I try to be at my best, to be firmly in command of my emotions. There's that icy coldness again. When I feel anger, as I said earlier, is when I lose control — like the time a speeding car nearly struck my daughter and I pounded my shoe on its hood."

"When have you been most afraid?"

Joyce hesitated briefly, and when she started to speak again, her voice was delicate, strained. "I confronted a gunman in the Ramada Inn at the airport in Los Angeles a couple of years ago," she began. "It was late at night, and because there was no bellman, I was walking alone through the corridor to find my room. I dragged behind me a big valise with wheels. The lights were out in the hallway."

She stopped.

"Suddenly," she began again, "there was a pistol against my head and a man threatened, 'I'm going to blow your head off.'"

"Did he know who you were?"

"No. It was dark and I kept my head down so I wouldn't see him."

"Why?"

"I wanted him to feel certain that he could not be identified. Otherwise he might just as easily pull the trigger. I was terrified, but I stayed in control of myself — icy again. In a monotone I told him: 'I keep my things very sloppily. I apologize. Some of my stuff is dirty.'

"My cash was stuffed throughout my possessions. I spread everything on the floor, kept apologizing, and I continued to give him my money as I found it. A dollar here, a dollar there. I moved very slowly, so as not to excite him. He was very jittery — and he had a very real pistol pressed against my temple. 'I'm leaving very early in the morning,' I assured him. 'You can see I'm not looking at you. I'm looking at the floor. I can't identify you.'

"Finally he pushed me into the bathroom.

" 'I'm leaving,' he said. 'If you come out, I'll blow your head off.'

"But he didn't leave.

"I felt truly vulnerable. A killer, a person I'd never know, could take my life at will. He tested me by standing quietly outside the bathroom door, pretending that he'd left, then he made sounds. *I couldn't lock the bathroom!* The latch was broken. Now that thought, I knew intellectually, made absolutely no sense. Even if I had been able to lock the door, he could have fired his pistol right through it — but the broken lock made me frantic. Also, I had a ring he hadn't seen — and I hid it. Why? I don't know. One of those things you do in terror. Was I going crazy? I reached my limit, and I burst out of the bathroom. He was gone."

"What did you do?"

"I called the police — and they came quickly."

"Did you know you were safe?"

"Then I did."

"How did you respond?"

"I broke down. I cried — and I cried off and on for the next two weeks."

As Joyce Brothers spoke, her voice growing more fragile as the story continued, I felt her pain. I could picture a bully terrorizing this gentle woman. What did not happen was a miracle. But what did happen, I knew, still hurt. Yet I also sensed something that had toughened — a resolve.

"I've faced embarrassment," Joyce told me, "and I've faced the possibility of being shot to death. For all of it, I feel even more strongly about taking risks."

"What would you advise?"

"First, let's accept that all of us can be hurt, that all of us can fail — and surely will at times. My experience in that Ramada Inn corridor was scary. Other vulnerabilities, though, like being embarrassed or risking love, can be terrifying too. I think we should keep a simple rule: *If we can take the worst, take the risk.*"

Risks would inspire far less worry if they followed the pattern of the quiz show, with each question leading predictably to the next, more difficult question. Risks are not rungs on a ladder, though. As I illustrated earlier, a risk is the ever-widening gap across an opening drawbridge. We don't step; we *leap* across the gap. That's why risks inspire fear. "My true risk," Joyce realized, "was the terrible embarrassment I imagined I'd suffer in a public failure . . . I had to confront the worst; I had to face my fear of embarrassment."

Joyce understood what was at risk. Thus she succeeded, as she herself observed, whether she correctly answered the $64,000 question or not. Sometimes in adolescence, though — as when I first joined the Marines, and also in the early career of the businessman we're about to meet — we are not aware there *is* a risk.

If I could find a top executive who was navigating through the center of an economic storm, I wondered, what manner of person would he be? What would I learn about risk-taking? Little can compare, I knew, to the first-person account of a seaman who sails through a hurricane; he knows the waves and the wind intimately, and because he has survived, he knows himself better than before.

I needed a leader — and I found him. Imagine the person in charge of a company with more than eight hundred thousand employees and $100 billion in sales, the largest company of its kind in the world and the largest of any kind in the United States, a company challenged daily in more than thirty countries and domestically by fierce competition, *rising* competition. I'm describing General Motors; its captain in these troubled seas, on a winter morning in 1987, was a soft-spoken man named Roger Smith, who at sixty-one was GM's chairman and chief executive officer.

We faced each other across the walnut desk in his beige corner office on the fourteenth floor of the General Motors Building in downtown Detroit. His hair was sandy, his complexion ruddy, and he wore gold-rimmed glasses, a gray plaid wool suit, a blue and black silk tie, and a tailored blue and white shirt, its French cuffs held by gold links. We had first met two years earlier in this same office, when I had sought his advice about an automotive project I wanted to undertake at *Parade* magazine. I remembered how candid and courteous he had been and how his advice, it turned out, had been wise. Looking at him now, I considered some of the risks he had taken. This slight, quiet financial executive had risen steadily through the ranks over three decades, and had surprised the industry with bold, sweeping changes shortly after he assumed the chairmanship — risks that included restructuring GM into two divisions from five, acquiring both Hughes Aircraft and Electronic Data Systems, virtually creating a whole new company called the Saturn project, and negotiating a mammoth joint venture with the Japanese automaker Toyota.

Four objects nearby, I suspected, hinted at the man who had held the office for six years. A few feet away was a salmon trophy awarded in Iceland in 1984; a toy Terex truck, a reminder of a project that had failed, rested next to a toy Pontiac Fiero, a project that had succeeded; and in a corner was a silver cup awarded in 1983 by the Automotive Hall of Fame to the "leader of the year."

"Roger," I asked, "where does risk-taking begin?"

"With a vision," he replied quickly, then added, "with an objective."

"How do you proceed?"

"I think," he began, "that once an objective is clear — and we should not proceed unless it *is* clear — we need to set reasonable goals to reach that objective. That's when we need to set down a strategy, to determine how we can achieve the goals that will lead us to our objective. In GM's case, we need to evaluate the impact not only on our divisions and the people who work in them, but on our suppliers, on our customers, and on our stockholders as well. Finally, after we understand the potential losses and gains, we come to the crunch: Do we do this?"

"How do *you* answer?"

"I know that when I face risk, I have to make a commitment at some point, a moment when reasoning and rational thought have been exhausted. Either I take the step, or I do not. This is when I have to ask, am I kidding myself? Am I manufacturing evidence because I really want to do this for reasons other than what I've said, or do I believe I should take the risk based on its own merit? In other words, is this right? If I convince myself that it is, that I've no hidden agenda, I go ahead. I've found it's important to know not only what I have at risk but *why*. We have to be honest with ourselves. If the risk is not to achieve the objective we've set, then frankly, we fail even if we succeed. The risks I lose sleep over are those where the chance for gain *and* loss is high. With a low-risk–high-gain situation, the decision seems easy; with a high-risk–high-gain situation, it's more difficult. The problem is, of course, that the same risks are weighed differently by different people. One fellow's low risk is another's high risk."

"Is that when you have to know in your heart what you'll do?"

"Yes," he answered, his voice rising enthusiastically. "You need to start with a sound philosophy. Risk-taking should not be an end unto itself. The guy who knows what he's doing when he takes a risk — not necessarily the one who succeeds — is the one to watch. I think the person to respect is the person who clearly understands the risk he's facing and takes the risk anyway. This is a tender subject with me, because it strikes, I believe, at our education. Schools should do more to help. In addition to having students memorize a poem — and in some cases *instead* of memorizing — our teachers should be emphasizing analysis. What makes a good poem as opposed to a bad poem? What makes a Picasso painting a classic, as contrasted to a Joe Schlock painting? We need to teach appreciation; we need to teach *judgment*. To be out there cracking new trails is more difficult — and more rewarding — than rolling down the highway. But in either case we need a direction, which is a basic, sound philosophy of living — in other words, judgment."

"Can we grow without changing?"

"No, I don't think we can. If we get in a rut, we'll wake up one morning and be sixty-five and we'll know no more than we did when we were twenty-five — and we'll be less secure. It's very easy to fall into this trap. It's natural for most people to avoid change, to avoid risk. I believe we must let go of our rock of security, whatever that rock may mean to each of us, and swim across the river of change. We grow in no other way. There is good news for those who try: The more risks we take, the more risks we're willing to take. It's not that it gets easier; it gets better."

"Roger," I asked, "you lead a company with almost a million employees, and decisions are often made in divisions by other executives and by committees, as they are in other large companies. But in the end, it is Roger Smith who must accept responsibility. Do you think about this in a personal way?"

"I try very hard not to. I have three and a half years to go as chairman of General Motors. I hope that I continue to make decisions as if I were going to be here for another twenty years. I carefully watched Tom Murphy, who preceded me as chairman, and in his last year I noticed he was intense.

" 'Is something bothering you?' I asked him one day.

" 'Yes,' he told me. 'It's this new plant we're building. I'm not going to be here when it comes on stream in two years.'

"You see, he cared — and when you care, those things get to you. I'm lucky, because I'll be chairman for ten years, as opposed to Tom and his immediate predecessors, who served shorter tenures. I think it's better to have a longer term. There's no escaping responsibility. It's right on my shoulders. I'll see the results of much of what we start."

"What about credit?"

"I have no aspirations to have a statue raised to me. More, I hope I never get in my own way. I've found myself wishing at times that no one would write about me or these decisions until I've been out of the job ten years. It's not that I can't cope with criticism. I can. I think, though, it will take a decade to know whether what we've done while I've been chairman is worth a damn. When I first became chairman, there seemed to be a shower of glowing profiles followed by Roger-bashing. I can't let either deflect me from doing what I think is right."

"Does the criticism hurt?"

"Sure it does — but it's more important to believe in your

heart that you've made your decisions for the right reasons. I remember my mother reminding me endlessly that I had to live with myself. Now I understand. She was wise. If I do my best and I succeed, I can share that. If I fail, I'm willing to accept responsibility. Again, we need a fundamental philosophy to act."

He sat silently. When he spoke again, his voice was buoyant.

"Walter," he said, "I'll share with you some advice my father gave me: 'Find something you really like,' he said, 'because you'll be doing it for a long time. If you do something that you don't like, no matter what you earn, you won't be worth a damn.' Today, after all these years at GM, I know that's literally true."

"How did you come to GM?"

He laughed.

"I had my bags packed," he said. "My tennis racket was stuffed in the back of my car, and my car was headed to California, because that's where my brother was, and so were all of my friends. They were in the aircraft business. My father, though, advised me to stop in at GM.

" 'Why?' I asked him.

" 'GM is the best-run, best-managed company in the world,' he told me.

" 'No,' I insisted, 'I'm going to California.'

"Ford Motor Company had wanted to put me in a training program, but I felt that after high school, four years of college, and two years of the navy, I wanted no more training. I wanted to work, to see if I had learned anything at all. Well, I finally acceded to my father's suggestion and reluctantly stopped by GM. I filled out an application, handed it to a woman through a window slot, and said to her, 'I'm sure you don't have any openings in finance.'

" 'Actually,' she replied, 'we have one job that we have not been able to fill.'

"I was directed upstairs to speak with a fellow named Chuck Sundlof, who I later realized was brilliant. 'You have good grades,' he noted, then added, 'but you're not qualified.'

" 'What did you say?'

" 'I said you're not qualified,' he repeated. 'It's a third-level foreign consolidation accounting job. It's very difficult. I'm sure you can't do it.'

"I was *shocked*. 'I've taken every course at Ann Arbor that Professor William Payton ever taught,' I argued. 'What do you mean I can't do it? I can do that job. Where is it? I'll work here for a month. If I can't do it, don't pay me.'

" 'Well,' he said, 'if you want to try it, then okay. We'll pay you for the month, though.'

"I started the job, and boy, I was in way over my head! In fact, I couldn't do it. I got on the phone with Professor Payton and pleaded, 'What the hell *is* this stuff? You didn't teach me this.'

" 'Roger,' he said, 'I'm teaching accounting for the average guy to go work in an average domestic corporation. I'll tell you what. You go to the books and you can learn what you need. You *can* do it. I *know* you can.'

"So I worked around the clock. My idea was to do the job for a month, prove myself, then tell Chuck Sundlof to shove it. The month came and went. By then I was too busy, too involved to quit. Thirty-eight years later, I'm still here."

"Do you fear failure?"

"I don't like failure, but I don't fear it. Fear of failure is like fear of falling. There's a risk you take if you climb a tree, isn't there?"

I nodded.

"If a grizzly was snapping at your heels, climbing a tree would seem like a small risk, wouldn't it?"

I nodded again.

"If you sit still, if you don't take risks, you're feeding the grizzly, not escaping it."

When Roger took his first job at General Motors, he was no wiser than I was when I enlisted in the military; clearly, neither one of us noticed that a drawbridge was widening at our feet. We were not brave or skilled risk-takers. We were instead mere adolescents, bursting forward, unseeing, to the other side.

Today, with the maturity and insight of decades of risk-taking, Roger convincingly declares, "It's important to know not only what I have at risk but *why*. We have to be honest with ourselves. If the risk is not to achieve the objective we've set, then frankly, we fail even if we succeed." When we decide who we are — *what I am*; *what I have*; *what I seem to be* — and when we frankly reveal to ourselves *why* we're facing a risk, as Roger discovered, we're learning how to be adults.

For me, as for Liz Smith, there was a moment, a point in time, when the world began to look somehow different. I was still a Marine and I was not quite nineteen years old.

This, I knew, was only *drill*; clearly, I had no chance. It was June 1963, and I was seventh in line to be interviewed for promotion to lance corporal.

"What are we supposed to do?" I asked the Marine standing behind me.

"Go through the motions," he suggested. "Where you and I are standing, the only thing we're going to make today is liberty — if we're lucky."

"Right," I agreed. "Maybe they'll get this over with fast, so we can change clothes and go to town."

"Now that's a *good* idea," he said, "because this stuff means nothing to me."

"Me neither," I lied.

The truth was, I *wanted* to be promoted. In a few days I'd be graduating from the last of the three electronics courses I had attended for almost a year. But the training, however useful, kept me off promotion lists; no one could be promoted while a student. I had become a private first class with twenty-one months in the Marine Corps. I also had passed high school and one-year college equivalency exams. In other words, when the studying had been most difficult for me, I had told myself I was learning how to be a better-educated PFC.

You, the Marine with all the schooling — sweep up the barracks.

It was worth more than that, I knew, but after almost two years, I was eager to be promoted. Not that I wasn't proud of what I had achieved. I knew that five times I had faced a challenge in the Marines, the most significant, of course, being the first — surviving, then graduating from Parris Island boot camp. Completing infantry training without a hitch also had given me confidence. Now, completing academics in these technical schools, particularly the math portion, since I had failed algebra, among other subjects, in high school, had me looking at myself differently. I remembered the day I had walked into the San Diego Marine Corps Recruit Depot, where the electronics school battalion was located, and my real concern as to whether I could pass. Meeting my classmates didn't help. Some had attended college; I was the only high school dropout.

Fortunately, the school assumed — correctly, in my case — that we knew *nothing*. We were taught everything we needed to know, from the most basic math to the more complex formulas necessary for understanding electronics. I finished eleventh in a class of twenty in my first course, eighth of seventeen in the second, and seventh of twenty-four in the third course. Originally I had hoped to pass, period. But sometime during the classes I began to want to do more than get by; I wanted to do well. The top third in our final course, I learned, would be interviewed for promotion, and three people would actually be promoted.

As I stood on line, I thought, well, I did my best. And if that's not good enough . . . it is *not* good enough, I admitted to myself. PFC Anderson, you're not going to be promoted today. Not Number *Seven*.

I asked Number Five, as he strode out, "What did they ask?"

"The lifer question," he said. " 'Are you going to stay in the Marine Corps?' "

"What did you tell them?"

He laughed loudly.

After Number Six, I was ordered into a small office in which sat a captain, a second lieutenant, and a first sergeant.

The captain spoke first: "Why are you here?"

"Sir," I said, "to be considered for promotion to lance corporal."

"Should you be promoted?"

"Yes, sir."

The captain glanced past the second lieutenant to the first sergeant.

"Why should we promote you," the sergeant asked, "when we can promote One, Two and Three?"

"I can't speak for them, first sergeant, only for me."

"Why *you*, then?"

"About a year and a half ago, I was a high school dropout. Today I have a high school GED, a one-year college GED, and I have successfully graduated from these three communications courses. I have proved myself."

The lieutenant interrupted. "What if you're *not* promoted?"

"I still have proved myself." And as I said it, I knew it was true. I *had* proved myself. Suddenly, it was as if a heavy seabag had been lifted from my shoulders; I was no longer nervous. Now I was going to enjoy this interview; I *had* succeeded.

"Are you going to stay in the Marine Corps?"

The *lifer* question. Ah-hah, I thought, I have to take a risk.

"Sir," I said, "I have more than two years to go. Would you believe me if I told you I was going to stay in?"

"Would *you* believe you?" the lieutenant interrupted.

"No," I said, "I would not. And something else —"

"What's that?"

"— I don't plan to stay in. And that's the truth. I have every intention of getting out of the Marine Corps, *sir.*"

The captain and the first sergeant dropped their heads, almost simultaneously. *Did they smile?*

The lieutenant, who seemed annoyed with me, asked, "Are you going to continue your education?"

"Yes, sir."

"Why?"

"Frankly, sir, after completing these courses, I think I can — and I'm going to."

"Do you know what you want to be?"

I paused.

"No, sir," I said, "I do not." I *was* enjoying myself, standing there telling the truth; the risk was worth it, whether I was promoted or not.

"Any idea?" the lieutenant pressed.

"I'm not sure. Sometimes I dream about writing, but I don't have the education. I'm going to give what I've learned here a good shot. Then I'll see."

"Anderson," said the captain, who had been silent, "you're very proud of yourself, aren't you?"

"Yes, sir, I am."

"And you don't expect to be promoted, do you?"

"No, sir."

"Good guess," the lieutenant blurted.

I thought I saw the captain's eyes flicker, but he continued as if the lieutenant had not spoken.

"Son," he said, "I know you're telling the truth. I hope, though, you're telling it for the right reasons, and not simply because you don't think you can be promoted anyway." He paused. "Let me tell you some of what your instructors say about you: You had the least education of any student in your class, and you should have finished last. Finishing seventh means you studied your butt off."

I listened silently, enjoying the report.

"And they also say you have trouble controlling your temper. Is that true?"

"No, sir," I replied, too quickly.

The captain arched an eyebrow.

The lieutenant smiled. He and I were destined to dislike each other intensely; at least, I was sure *I* disliked *him*.

"Are you certain?" asked the first sergeant, his face serious.

"Sir," I added, "I'm determined — no, enthusiastic —" I was searching for a word. "Look, I have a temper, but I do control it. You don't know how hard I work to keep my temper —"

The captain interrupted. "What would you like to say to the lieutenant here?"

The lieutenant looked perplexed.

I paused.

"I don't believe we think much of each other, sir."

"Anderson, that's not what I asked you."

"I have nothing to say to the lieutenant," I replied evenly, and that was true.

"If you're promoted to lance corporal," the first sergeant said, "the next step is corporal, then maybe even sergeant. Are you ready to be an NCO?"

"Yes, sir, I am."

"Would you be a *good* NCO?" the lieutenant asked.

"Yes, sir," I said, understanding clearly that I wouldn't have the opportunity this time around.

"Dismissed," the first sergeant said.

"How was it?" Number Eight asked as I walked past him.

"Not bad," I said, "but watch out for the lieutenant."

"Did you make it?" he asked. "Are you going to be promoted?"

"You've got to be kidding," I said, laughing loudly. "Not today."

Two hours later I got a call from a woman Marine named Linda whom I had dated and who worked in the office. "Andy," she confided, using my nickname, "you're a lance corporal!"

"Me?"

"No kidding!" she insisted. "I've got their notes right here. All three put you right on top."

"Even the lieutenant?"

"Andy," she said, perplexed by my question, "*he* recommended you."

Within six months I was promoted again, to corporal. Then in 1965, while serving in Vietnam, I was promoted one more time, to sergeant. Eventually, I'd be honorably discharged from the Marine Corps. I'd land a job on a small newspaper, and I'd work full-time and attend school full-time. In a few years, I would be chosen to be editor and general manager of the newspaper on which I had started my career, the *Reporter Dispatch* in White Plains, New York. I would become an investigative reporter, an author, a newspaper editor, and later, the editor of *Parade* magazine. I'd teach as an adjunct professor of psychology and sociology, and I'd also be elected chairman of the board of trustees of one of the two colleges from which I would graduate. One day I'd even be offered the presidency of a multimillion-dollar corporation. I would meet and become friends with some of the brightest and most noble people on earth. Yet as I recall this promotion to lance corporal, even after twenty-five years, I know that no achievement has moved me more. Perhaps if I had not been promoted, my life would have unfolded in precisely the same way; maybe I'd be writing this book, minus only this memory. I believe, though, that if I had to choose an instant in time when the world turned for me, it would be then, at the San Diego Marine Corps Recruit Depot — the day three men believed in me.

Part Three

"HOW MUCH WATER'S in the stream?" asks the teacher of his fourth grade class.

The room goes silent as a cave.

"Doesn't *anyone* know?"

A single arm rises in the last row.

"I know!" volunteers the eager student, his hand still in the air.

"Are you sure?" asks the teacher, puzzled.

The student nods.

"Yes!" he says. "I've measured it."

"You've *measured* it?"

"Yes," the little boy replies, his voice very serious, "I sure have."

"How much then?"

"Four yardsticks!" exclaims the student.

Unlike this fourth grader, we know we can't measure volume with a ruler — but regularly we help foster a measure almost as ambiguous. We insist that our children start kindergarten at a particular time in their lives, and we expect them to graduate from high school in their middle to late teens. Our companies, when not prevented by labor laws from insisting on mandatory retirement, create programs to encourage those of a particular age — often as young as fifty-five — to leave. Why? We expect, and frequently we require, people of certain ages to behave as we think they should. How old must a person be to purchase liquor? So many times we hear "Act your age," which is what is told to the ten-year-old schoolgirl as she paints her face with gooey globs of thick makeup, slips on her mother's high heels, and lights a Marlboro, and it's the advice given to her grandfather as he mounts his Harley-Davidson motorcycle, picks up his teenage girlfriend, then scoots off to the Krypton disco. We've learned to gauge our lives, our progress, often our value as human beings, by our age — and no measure known to mankind has been more imprecise. Truly, we've laid a yardstick over a stream.

To master the process of risk-taking in our lives, however, we must examine another measure of maturity, one that will help us define what it really means to be adult. Let's begin with a man who lives his dream.

I first met Irving Wallace during the fall of 1980, in the den of his Brentwood, California, home. I was there to suggest that he, his daughter, Amy, and his son, David, write a column of unusual facts for *Parade*, the magazine of which I had only recently become editor. I was . . . well, *very* enthusiastic, and tried my best to be persuasive. Yet although Irving was cordial and warm, he was noncommittal.

Finally I said, "You have *almost* everything a writer could want in his life."

I had his attention. He was, after all, one of the most prosperous novelists *ever*.

"Almost?" he asked.

"Yes," I said, "you're just missing one thing."

"What's that?"

In for a penny, I thought, in for a pound. I wonder if he

has a sense of humor. "You're missing *me*," I replied, "as your editor."

He laughed loudly, and so did I. I'm sure it was then, in that delightful moment when this enormously successful author was so gracious and good-humored with a very vulnerable young editor, that I knew I had made a friend.

Shortly before Christmas of that same year, he called to say that he and his children would do the column I had proposed.

"We'll try it for a year," he promised, "and we'll call it *Significa*."

"Wonderful," I told him.

The column continued not for one but for three years, and it eventually was published as a book — and Irving, his wife, Sylvia, and David and Amy remain my friends for life. So when I called Irving during the winter of 1987 to ask him to sit for an interview for this book, I expected a quick reply.

"Yes," he said.

This time we sat next to each other at a restaurant, La Scala, on Santa Monica Boulevard in Beverly Hills. Irving was seventy-one, the author of more than thirty-five popular novels and nonfiction books, including *The Chapman Report*, *The Prize*, *The Plot*, *The Man*, and *The Word*, and co-author with his children of *The Book of Lists*, *The People's Almanac*, and *The Two*. His large, wide-set brown eyes seemed to have a will of their own, twinkling as he spoke; his voice was a deep, distinctive, commanding baritone. Handsome, with thick, wavy, steel-gray hair, he had presence, a natural, unaffected charisma.

I had eagerly looked forward to this dinner. Irving, like *Roots* author Alex Haley, is as good a storyteller in person as he is in print — if only I could get him started.

"What," I asked, "has been your greatest risk?"

"To do with my life what I really wanted to," he said. "I worked at the movie studios for ten years, but the more money

I made, the more I hated it. I didn't like having an employer, keeping hours, or writing as part of some committee. I was convinced — I'm still convinced! — that the only great book to come out of a committee was the King James Bible. But I was earning a thousand dollars a week, which was a great deal in the fifties. And I was moving up in the movie industry. Yet, as I've said, I was in agony. I felt I'd go insane with all these characters in the movie business telling me what to write. I *hated* it — but I needed the money. I had to support my family."

"What was your dream?"

"All my life I wanted to do one thing, and that was to write books. No boss, nobody to touch my work in a basic way . . . *to say what I wanted to say in the world.*"

"But?"

"But how could I quit when I was earning so much, when we had two children?"

"What did you do?"

"One night I came home and sat at the kitchen table with my wife, and I said, 'Sylvia, I want to quit the movies to write books. I know that's a big risk — I'm making a thousand dollars a week, and the most I've made on any of the four books that I've written so far is five thousand dollars — but I promise I'll write three books a year, under different names if I have to, to earn enough. What do you think?'

" 'Good,' she told me, 'because I'd rather own less than to see you go crazy, being so upset all the time. You come home from the studio every day and you have a couple of drinks, and you know, that's no way to live your life. Your life is just on its way. Do what you need to do.'

"At the time — it was 1958, and I was forty-two — I was writing a second novel on the side, after work and on weekends. I had written a hundred pages. But I had no more money. It happened then that I received a call from a paperback publisher named Victor Weybright, who was the head of New American Library. He had read a book I'd written called *The Fabulous Showman*, the life of P. T. Barnum, and he wanted to reprint it. He said, 'I liked your writing and I'd like to meet with you.'

"He'd be in California shortly, he told me, and he'd be staying at the Beverly Hills Hotel.

"This, I told myself, was my moment of truth. We met in the hotel.

" 'I hear you have two ideas for books,' he said.

" 'Yes,' I said.

" 'Tell me about both,' he suggested, 'five minutes each.'

"I told him about the novel first, which centered on a sex survey taken in West Los Angeles. I didn't mention that I had already written one hundred pages. He was silent. Then I told him about a nonfiction book I planned, *The Twenty-Seventh Wife*, which would be the story of Brigham Young's last wife in polygamy, an actress who left her husband and campaigned against multiple marriage.

" 'Look,' he said, 'the novel sounds like a good idea, though I don't know what you can do in fiction. You've only written one novel.'

"I waited.

" '*The Twenty-Seventh Wife*, though, is a *brilliant* idea . . .'

"Still I waited, the long seconds passing.

" 'In any case, you have two books . . .'

"I thought, 'Did he say *two* books?'

" 'All right,' he asked. 'What do you need to write them?'

"What, I worried, do I ask for? I would be lucky to get five thousand dollars. Well, as I said, this was my moment of truth. 'I need twenty-five thousand dollars,' I told him.

" 'You have a deal,' he said. 'I want to buy the paperback rights.'

"We shook hands. I remember I hurried downstairs, grabbed a phone, and called Sylvia.

" 'I'm through with movies forever!' I announced. She was delighted.

"Next, I called my Hollywood agent, who was not delighted. 'Irving,' he said, 'you cannot do this. You're earning a thousand dollars a week, and I have two big jobs scheduled for you that will make you a millionaire. These books are small potatoes. You already earn in six months what they're giving you for two books. Ridiculous! For twelve and a half thousand dollars a book, you're going to give up a career and certain riches?'

" 'Yes,' I said, 'I am.'

" 'But why?'

" 'Because I have to live with myself,' I said, 'and be free to say the things I want to say.'

" 'Are you sure?' he asked.

"I was sure — and the following Monday I sat down in front of my typewriter and I started page 101 of my novel. I knew I had twelve thousand and five hundred dollars coming in. I dreamed about writing the Great American Novel. I was free!

"Some months later, when I had just finished typing page 200, my agent called again. 'The two deals I told you about,' he announced, 'one with Paramount and the other with Twentieth Century-Fox — they just came in. Stop this book nonsense now. It's time to go back to work. You're no kid. You have a family. Do what's right for them. No more thousand-dollar weeks. Now you'll make real money. Irving, you're going to be rich. What do you say?'

"I had thought my meeting with Weybright was my moment of truth. Now I realized it wasn't. This phone call was my moment of truth. 'No,' I said."

"How did you feel?"

"I remember," he replied, "taking a deep breath."

We both laughed.

"What happened next?"

"Later, when I finished the novel, I packaged it in a box and mailed it to my New York literary agent, Paul Reynolds. He called me quickly. 'Irving,' he said, 'this is kind of shameful. It's a fictional sex survey on women's lives. Are you sure you want to keep your name on it?'

" 'Of course I want to keep my name on it,' I told him. 'I'm proud of it!'

" 'Well, all right then,' he said. 'We'll put it out for an early auction to hardcover publishers.' The paperback rights had been purchased earlier by Victor Weybright, of course, for the twelve thousand five hundred.

"Well, seven publishing houses bid. My former publisher, Alfred Knopf, heard about the auction and called each bidder. 'You're my friend,' he said, 'but if you have anything to do with Wallace or that book' — which he had not read — 'I'll have nothing to do with you.'

"Knopf was a powerful and a difficult man. He was annoyed, I'm sure, that I had left his publishing house to sell at an auction. Two of the seven publishers, though, told him to go to hell. One was Doubleday and the other was Simon and Schuster.

"Paul Reynolds called with the good news — and a dilemma. Both publishers offered exactly the same advance, he told me, which was twenty-five thousand dollars.

"I was thrilled. I thought to myself that maybe I had lost the million dollars I might have earned writing movie scripts, as my Hollywood agent had warned, but I *had* written my novel, and somebody not only wanted to publish it, they were willing to defy Alfred Knopf. At Paul's suggestion we went with Simon and Schuster, and it became my publishing house for the next quarter of a century."

"Irving," I asked, "what was the title of that novel?"

He smiled. *"The Chapman Report,"* he said.

I knew that *The Chapman Report* not only had become a major best-seller — more than four million copies were sold in the United States alone — but it had been made into a movie as well.

"Darryl F. Zanuck paid one hundred and seventy-five thousand dollars for the movie rights," Irving reported, "and —"

"And?" I asked.

"— and then I knew I was free."

"You completed *The Twenty-Seventh Wife?*"

"Yes."

"What came next?"

"The Prize."

"Another best-seller — and next?"

"The Three Sirens."

"And?"

"The Man."

"My favorite!"

We both laughed.

"Irving," I said, "nearly two hundred *million* copies of your novels have now been sold throughout the world. You've become one of the planet's five most popular contemporary authors. What was the reaction among those with whom you had worked at the studios?"

"Joy and sadness. Several of the scriptwriters had told me that I was crazy — particularly those who were as unhappy working for the studios as I had been. When it became apparent in 1960 that *The Chapman Report* was a success, some of these former co-workers made me a larger-than-life figure — a legend — but I knew who I was."

"And who was that?"

"Merely a man who had taken a risk. I had gambled. Now

I look at the field of movie scriptwriting and I see that those who did not take risks, who continued to do what they secretly disliked, can't get jobs today. They thought they had security, but the security was an illusion. Instead, for years some have had to get facelifts — can you imagine that? — to try to appear younger, because they have to have a more youthful look when they seek studio work."

"How did *you* regard your good fortune?"

"I was overjoyed. I was doing what I really wanted to do, and that was to write novels."

"Success, though, had its surprises, didn't it?"

He nodded.

"It sure did," he said. "*The Chapman Report* was a sensation, and then *The Prize* was even bigger. Then, when I started to write *The Three Sirens*, a producer pledged, 'Sight unseen, I'll pay you half a million dollars for the movie rights to your new novel.' My agent, understandably, didn't believe this, and he demanded that the producer bring to his office a certified check for five hundred thousand dollars. The producer arrived, the check in hand. And I hadn't even shown him the book yet!

"A few days later, I was in the midst of a long interview with the Associated Press and I got a dizzy spell. For the next year I suffered from imbalance. I couldn't walk a few feet without grasping onto something for support. I visited specialists — every type of doctor you can imagine. Finally one diagnosed me correctly. 'Irving,' he said, 'all this attention and success has gone to your head. There's nothing organically wrong with you. Start another book, go to Europe. Forget these rewards. This is all so heady, it's literally making you dizzy.' "

"Did you take his advice?"

"Yes. I regained some perspective, and the dizzy spells ended."

"Is that when you started to write *The Man*?"

He nodded.

"Irving," I asked, "how did your publisher like the idea of your writing a novel about a black man becoming president of the United States?"

"The publisher told me, 'People aren't ready to read a book like this.'

" 'I know how to write it,' I argued.

" 'We're not going to tell you what to write,' the editors said, warning me, 'but it's very dangerous.' "

"Were you concerned?"

"Sure."

"Why did you go ahead?"

He paused. "I've thought about that," he said, his words coming slowly. "I wrote *The Man* because I believed in the idea of the book . . . and finally I remembered why I had left the movie business: *to say what I wanted to say in the world.* This then, in a sense, was another moment of truth, another risk for me. Would I say what I wanted to say?"

"And you did?"

"Yes."

"And how did you feel when *The Man* became a best-seller?"

"I was very happy," he replied, "but I knew that writing *The Man* was my real success. I had kept my word to myself."

As he spoke, I was reminded of the first time I had met Irving Wallace — of his cordiality, his warmth, his generosity, when we sat in his den and I thought, *this* is a writer's home. I remembered details: he was a collector, having acquired the work of artists such as Gauguin, Modigliani, Matisse, Picasso, and Chagall, hundreds of autographed photographs and letters of historically important people, priceless manuscripts, electronic gadgets, furnishings and oddities, many first editions of famous books.

"Irving," I had asked, "why do you collect the materials and work of so many talented people?"

"To make them real to me," he had said. "We go to a museum and we can't touch the stuff. It can be hard to believe people like Washington and Jefferson and Lincoln and Poe really existed; it's hard to *touch* them. But when I have something of theirs in my hand, then they're real. I can dream with them. I have a chair that belonged to Charles Dickens, Arthur Conan Doyle's traveling desk, Lewis Carroll's armchair — and I sit in that chair and I wonder, why can't I write *Alice in Wonderland*? And I talk to myself as if they're there. It's exciting to touch some part of the great people of our past, like the first page of one of Henry David Thoreau's writings."

"What do you most treasure?"

"Of all I've collected?"

"Yes."

"I treasure most an autographed manuscript written in pen on cheap ruled paper, the words of a former slave who became a diplomat, a writer, an adviser to President Lincoln. I used it as an epigraph to *The Man*." Then he had showed me the paper:

In a composite Nation like ours, made up of almost every variety of the human family, there should be, as before the Law, no rich, no poor, no high, no low, no black, no white, but one country, one citizenship, equal rights and a common destiny for all.

A Government that cannot or does not protect the humblest citizen in his right to life, Liberty and the pursuit of happiness, should be reformed or overthrown, without delay.

Frederick Douglass

Washington D.C.   Oct. 20, 1883

"Can you feel the life in those words?" Irving asked me.
"Yes," I said, "I can."

Picture yourself in front of a mirror fogged with steam. Wipe away the moisture. Do you see yourself? Now rub that mirror, rub it hard. The silver reflection disappears — and the glass is a window. When the mirrors of our minds become windows, when we see — and care — beyond ourselves, when we see and learn from others, only then do we become adults.

Children learn when to trust; adolescents search for identity; adults see beyond themselves.

As children, we begin to wipe away the moisture from the mirror. In adolescence, we stare at the reflection. It is our acceptance of who we are, blemishes and all, that allows us to wipe away the silver, to become adult. "I knew who I was," Irving said, and with that insight he saw the world as it really is.

Without a declaration similar to Irving's, risk-taking may be little more than a toss of the dice. The world is a hard and unpredictable arena. Only when we can say with conviction *I accept who I am* are we adequately prepared to look beyond ourselves, to face risk — and loss — as an adult.

Consider the experience of a caring, talented woman who couldn't make a particular risk come out as she had hoped, no matter how hard she tried.

She had been the fiftieth Miss America, the first lady of Kentucky, this country's most successful woman sportscaster, and the co-host of *The NFL Today*, *Candid Camera*, and *The Miss America Pageant*, and when she waved to me across the Grill Room of the Four Seasons restaurant in Manhattan on a steamy summer evening in 1987, I had to remind myself that Phyllis George Brown also had endured disappointment, loss, and burning criticism. She was, I knew, a risk-taker in every sense of the word, and she had agreed to discuss with me not only her varied achievements but also her doomed tenure as co-anchor of *The CBS Morning News* in 1985, a job that paid nearly a million dollars a year but that she had not discussed publicly since the project had failed two years earlier.

Now, as she sat across from me — thirty-seven years old, a mother of two, slender, animated, vivacious in a stylish black silk top and skirt, simple silver and pearl earrings, a silver and pearl pin at her neck, her brown hair swept high off her face, her dark brown eyes wide, expressive — I remembered how she had surprised me when we spoke for the first time over the phone in April. I was sure from my research that in her life, in its highs and its lows, much could be learned about risk; I was less sure that I could persuade her to talk about it. After all, though we had mutual friends, we had not met.

"Phyllis," I said on the phone, "I want to ask you about becoming Miss America, but I'd also like you to discuss what you experienced at CBS."

She hesitated.

"I haven't talked about that," she told me.

"I know, but your experience, what you've learned, can help many people."

The line was quiet for another second or two.

"Maybe you're right," she said.

Now, seated together months later in the Grill Room, Phyllis recalled, "I was nineteen when I entered the Miss Texas pageant for the first time. I represented my hometown as Miss Denton. I felt honored! I loved my small town. When I was named Miss Congeniality, I was thrilled, because that meant the other girls liked me — and that too was important to me. It turned out I also won the swimsuit, the evening gown, and the talent competitions and did very well in my interview — and I could sense that I was a favorite of the audience. Then came the announcement of Miss Texas."

"How did you place?" I asked.

"I was second runner-up," she said.

"What did you feel?"

"You have to understand," she replied, her words slow and even, "I was a young girl from a little town who had tried as hard as she could in a big city contest — and after winning those other competitions, I really thought I would be crowned Miss Texas. I was crushed."

"What did you do?"

"I vowed I'd never enter another contest," she said.

"But you did?"

"Yes," she replied, laughing, "and in a funny way, quite by accident. The following year I was encouraged by several people to compete again, but I declined. I remembered the disappointment all too well. Also, my life was full. I was an educational speech major, doing my student teaching, and I lived in a sorority house on campus. I had a boyfriend. 'No,' I declared, 'not again, not me.' My parents even wrote a note explaining that I would not be a contestant. That was that, I thought.

"Then, one Friday night I happened to drive to my home in Denton to pick up some clothes. My father was asleep on the couch and my mother was playing bridge when the phone rang, so I answered it — a simple act that changed my life. The call was from an official of the Miss Texas contest. He told me that the preliminaries for Miss Dallas were being held the very next day, and he suggested that I enter. I told him no, but he wouldn't give up. He really knew how to make a case. 'Look,' he argued, 'if you enter, the worst is that you'll pick up some scholarship money.' That hit home. The scholarship award I had received the year before had, in fact, been important to me and my family. He was very persuasive. I announced, much to my parents' astonishment, 'I'll be there tomorrow.' Now, as I look back over these years, I think about how different my life might have been if I had not returned to my home in Denton that Friday night, or taken that call, or if I had said no.

"The next morning I barely made the cut. I was out of shape. I hadn't played the piano in a year. The judges, though, eventually picked me as Miss Dallas and told me that if I worked at it, I could be Miss Texas. They apparently had seen me the year before; in fact, they told me, 'Phyllis, we know you're better than you look today.' I felt encouraged, and I started to exercise again, swimming and bicycling. I worked up a new song, a medley of "Raindrops Keep Fallin' On My Head" and "Promises, Promises." I felt good about myself. I enjoyed playing the piano again, and I liked the way I looked after all the exercise. I realized too I was a step up from the previous year — because I had lost, I had experience. I remember someone asking me what I thought was an odd question: 'Do you want to be Miss Congeniality, or do you want to win?' I wondered, what does one have to do with the other? You can't please everyone all the time.

"Well, it turned out I didn't win Miss Congeniality, but I did win the Miss Texas title, which meant that I would be in the 1971 Miss America competition. I promised myself I'd go for broke; I would do my best. I had a goal — well, more a wish or a dream than a goal: I wanted to make the top ten. But if I didn't make it, I knew that this time I wouldn't be hurt, because just being in the Miss America contest was enough for me. Every year, like millions of other young girls across America, I had watched the Miss America program on television with my mother. I had walked around with books on my head to achieve perfect posture, and probably did dozens of silly things that every girl thinks might make a difference. I was thrilled: Phyllis George from Denton, Texas, was on her way to Atlantic City!

"Talent was important in the Miss America contest — it counted fifty percent, in fact. And though I played my heart out, unlike in the two Texas contests, I didn't win the talent competition. Then, the following night, to my surprise, I won the swimsuit competition. Next came the choosing of the top ten. I waited.

"They called my name — and I went numb. It was as if I were disembodied. I was asked some questions from my biography, and I heard my voice answer. Things seemed fuzzy, out of focus. A first runner-up was announced — but she wasn't me. Miss South Carolina leaned over, smiled, and whispered, 'The Lord be with you.' Then I won.

"I couldn't believe it. I was transfixed. There were a lot of voices, and somebody placed a robe on me, then a banner, then a crown, a special gold crown because it was the fiftieth anniversary of Miss America. Here was my big moment!"

"And," I interrupted, "the world came unglued."

"Did it ever!" she said. "When I nodded to the judges to say thank you, the crown wobbled, slid from my head, and landed on my foot, with stones popping out and spilling all over the runway. I leaned to retrieve the crown and the robe fell to my elbows, the banner came unpinned, the flowers scrunched in my hands. I remember standing there humiliated at the end of the runway for what seemed an eternity, devastated because I had dropped the crown. Finally they signaled me to turn around, and I turned around. I was embarrassed beyond words. Not only was I clumsy, I was clumsy for all the world to see.

"Two nights later I was to appear on the Johnny Carson show. The producers suggested that I wear my gown and crown, but I asked if I could simply wear a cocktail dress. When I stepped out, Johnny asked me good-naturedly whether I had forgotten my crown or whether I was worried that I might drop it again. I had a choice. I could relive my embarrassment and be humiliated again, or I could have some fun.

"Fortunately, I made the right choice.

" 'I was afraid I couldn't keep it on my head!' I blurted, and everyone, including me, laughed. It was funny — and it was true. I'm sure that's why Johnny and I developed a comfortable rapport and I was asked to appear again on his show.

"In time that painful moment of embarrassment even became a positive thing, distinguishing me from other Miss Americas. Folks forgot the fiftieth anniversary. But you know what they remember? Me, the klutz: 'I'm the one who dropped the crown.'

" 'Oh, you're Phyllis George!' "

She laughed — and I realized it was time to ask the question Phyllis would find the most difficult to answer. "What happened at CBS?"

She didn't flinch.

"It started with *Good Morning America* on ABC," she said. "I filled in for Joan Lunden a couple of times. The people who produced the show made me feel comfortable, welcome, and I got along easily with the co-host, David Hartman. It was a good time for me and my family. John and I and our two young children were enjoying our life in Kentucky. Because *Good Morning America* was Joan and David's show and my role as a guest host was limited to an occasional fill-in, a plane trip to New York, I felt very little pressure. Then . . ." She paused.

"Some of the executives at CBS must have noticed that the ratings seemed to hold up for ABC when I subbed for Joan. Their show, *The CBS Morning News*, was third behind ABC's *Good Morning America* and NBC's *Today*. Apparently they decided I was their solution, or a part of it. So I was asked to be guest host one week, and then a second week. They seemed to be pleased with what they saw.

"I was less sure. *Good Morning America* had a personality — it was an upbeat, positive type of show. *The CBS Morning News*, in contrast, was what its title said it was — a news report. When CBS approached me, I found myself resisting. This was no small decision in my life. I was well aware that this was a major move for me, personally and professionally. I knew if I agreed to do the show, which would be a full-time job, I'd have to ask my family to move to New York. Also, I wasn't entirely sure from what I had seen of *The CBS Morning News* that I could fit in, that I could handle the assignment well. After all, reporting hard news was not my background."

"Was there anything to caution you?" I asked.

"Yes," she said, nodding. "I remember a friend in broadcasting warning me that I would be, in her words, 'boarding the *Titanic*' and that no one had succeeded — and, she insisted, no one could succeed — on *The CBS Morning News*."

"Why did you take the risk?"

"First," she replied, "it seemed like a genuine opportunity for me to grow. I thought I could really challenge myself — plus my experience at *Good Morning America* gave me confidence. Then two important things happened to convince me to say yes. My husband told me, 'Look, Phyllis, you came to Kentucky for us. If you'd like to tackle this, we'll go to New York for you.' And the CBS executives made a promise: 'The show,' I was told, 'will be built around you, Phyllis. We're going to be competitive in the mornings now. *CBS Morning News* will be different. Expect our support. We'll be there to help.'"

"That did it?"

"That did it! If CBS is going to make that large an investment in time and money and trust in me, I thought, if they are going to build the show around what they feel are my strengths, if I have my family's support, how can I say no? Full steam ahead!"

She paused again, took a deep breath, put her hand to her chin.

"I haven't really talked about this," she said, dropping her hand back to her lap, "but I will, because I believe in the message of your book.

"After a short time, I realized that the pledge to reshape the show was hollow. Simply put, *The CBS Morning News* would remain *The CBS Morning News*, with me as an anchor. I was stuck. Although I was geared to entertainment, to personality interviews and human interest stories, the show remained basically hard news. Somehow my presence and a new set, it was hoped, would accomplish what three decades of effort had failed to achieve and rescue CBS from the cellar in those morning hours. Of course, it didn't. And I struggled. Don't complain, I told myself, don't explain — and most important, don't give up."

She hesitated.

"Phyllis," I said, "I've read the criticism. It was scathing, as if your mere presence on *The CBS Morning News* was offensive. The reviews were bitter."

"That's true," she said, "and the criticism hurt. I can't pretend it didn't. It hurt a lot, particularly because I tried so hard. What I didn't grasp at the time was that I was in a company about to go to war with itself. Stock ownership and top management were going to change dramatically, with high-executive firings and large-scale layoffs. Divisions were going to be sold off. And *CBS Morning News*, after one more set of anchors, would be canceled."

"Phyllis, why did it fall apart?"

"Now that I understand what was to follow, I think the top people at CBS were sincere when they promised me a new show, but they lost their nerve when faced with criticism from corporate old-timers: Why is Phyllis George here? What does she know? How can our network, the network that lives in the shadow of the great Edward R. Murrow, allow a beauty queen, a sportscaster, a governor's wife, in the news department? So they went halfway, creating that new set and slightly softening but not fundamentally changing the focus of the report and its approach to news. It was *The Phyllis-George-Doing-the-CBS-Morning-News-Show*. I became simply a replacement, one more in a long list over three decades. And despite my years as a sportscaster and other television experience, I had not been out in the trenches, like most of my predecessors, covering news events — so I was an easy and obvious target. In a very visible way, I became a symbol of the new versus the old. Only the new got cold feet — and they broke their promise."

"What did you do?"

"Well, at first I wondered, what *can* I do? I knew complaining would get me nowhere. Who could I complain to, those who hadn't kept their word? My critics? No, it was up to me. I had been working more than fourteen hours every day. I tried to work harder. I studied my notes until ten P.M., then stumbled out of bed four hours later to read more notes to prepare myself for the morning broadcast. I wanted so badly to do well. After two months of feeling alone and frustrated, I finally began to ask myself, why am I here?"

"But you didn't quit?"

"No," she said, "not at first. I kept at it. Some of it I loved, like interviewing Jeane Kirkpatrick, Sherry Lansing, and Cathy Black for a series called 'Women of Influence.' But most of it was a hard climb.

"Ironically, it was Walter Cronkite, the very first anchor of *The CBS Morning News*, who helped me to understand what was happening.

" 'Phyllis,' he told me, 'they didn't know what they wanted in that broadcast when I was the first to do it thirty-three years ago — and they still don't today.' That was when I really began to understand that as long as it was called *The CBS Morning News*, it would be hard news, period. And that's not me. Perhaps in time I could have learned to be a skilled journalist in their tradition, but I don't think I have the edge, the necessary skepticism to go with it. I've conducted some interesting interviews in my career and provoked quotable responses, but I've never been confrontational. That's not who I am. I do my best work when I'm able to put the subject at ease, when we're comfortable with each other."

She paused, then said, "I had to leave *The CBS Morning News*."

"When did you decide that it was over?" I asked.

"It was hard to get to that point," she replied. "It was difficult for me to admit to myself, after I had seemed to succeed at so many other challenges, that I was not going to succeed again. It was the wrong format for me. Also, we had moved our family from Kentucky, and we had made other commitments. But about eight months after I had started on *The CBS Morning News*, the day before a two-week vacation, I told my husband, 'This is not working. It's over, John. I won't enjoy this vacation unless I talk to someone at CBS.' He encouraged me to do it, and I did.

"I knew I had to initiate the talk. I had to encourage the decision-makers at CBS to reach a conclusion that seemed inescapable to me. It was no longer whether I would leave, but when. I hoped to help management make the decision sooner rather than later. So I made an appointment with an executive vice president, sat down, and said, 'Let's look at what we have here: a show that doesn't work. The ratings are better, but they are not soaring. No one knows what we're supposed to be, news or entertainment. Nearly every day I'm criticized as a person who shouldn't be doing what she's doing. If you're not going to make the necessary changes to make it work for me, then you need someone else, and you need a clear idea of what *The CBS Morning News* should be. Let's agree that we all started out with the best intentions but that this project hasn't worked as well as we hoped it would.' "

"What followed?"

"Two weeks later, when my vacation ended, a network executive called me in Kentucky and told me, 'Phyllis, we're going to keep it a hard news show.' That was it; it was over. The decision had been made. I'd be replaced."

"How did you feel?"

"Tremendously relieved," she said, "and at the same time disappointed and hurt. I wasn't as brave as my words may sound. I'm only human. I was very upset."

"Do you have regrets?"

"No," she said, "I'm glad I took the risk. And I'm glad I walked away. I know now I'm stronger for having done both. I learned if you don't take a risk, you don't grow. If you don't grow, you can't be satisfied. If you're not satisfied, you can't be happy. You have the right to be happy."

"Did you learn anything more?"

"Yes," she replied, "quite a bit about myself. Had I not picked up that telephone years ago in Denton, Texas, and risked failure, I would never have gone to Atlantic City. And what if I had won that Miss Texas pageant the year before, what if I had succeeded then? I doubt that I would ever have been Miss America. Some may say that my biggest risk was entering a male-dominated arena, the world of sportscasting. In the beginning I was signed for a thirteen-week option only, but it was renewed. In fact, I was at *CBS Sports* for ten years, ten incredibly fulfilling years — and I liked being a pioneer for women in sportscasting. It seems like all my life I've moved from one risk to another.

"Look, *The CBS Morning News* didn't work out for me, but I survived. A door closed, but a window opened. Personally, I have more time with my children, which I treasure. Professionally, I have a clearer view of my strengths and I know where I can improve — and I will. That doesn't mean the whole episode wasn't difficult, but the experience has strengthened me. I'd feel different, of course, if I had hurt someone else, but I was the only one hurt. Perhaps the greatest lesson in this for me, and maybe for others, is that a risk doesn't have to succeed to be valuable. You grow stronger even when risks don't work out. How sad I would be today if I had not tried. It was a great opportunity. Something else —"

"What is that?"

"— we *do* survive. Everything doesn't come tumbling down because of something Phyllis George or Walter Anderson or anyone tries. As important as our risks are to us — and my CBS experience was certainly public — the world is not focused on us. Life goes on. Unless you've truly risked your life, in the end no risk is that large. Will people still like you if you fail? Of course they will. I remember how a cabdriver whom I'd never met before greeted me with a loud 'Hi, Phyllis! How're you doing, kid?' only a couple of days after the announcement that I'd left CBS. And I remember laughing. Nothing changes, I thought to myself. Well, of course, some things do change, for the better. We do get other chances in life, and we're better prepared for them the next time. I'm starting a new business now — a company called Chicken by George! — and who knows what risks lie ahead?"

"Would you return to television?"

"Yes," she said.

"When?" I asked.

"At the first good risk," she replied, laughing. "And you know, that's true!"

When Phyllis first began to think about *The CBS Morning News*, a hard question emerged: "Could this new challenge be an opportunity for me to grow?" This recognition that growth was possible, perhaps desirable, became her positive loss. Her practical losses — uprooting her family from Kentucky, disrupting her stable life with career pressures — were tougher to accept, but as she said, "Two important things happened to convince me to say yes. My husband told me, 'Look, Phyllis, you came to Kentucky for us. If you'd like to tackle this, we'll go to New York for you.' And the CBS executives made a promise: 'The show,' I was told, 'will be built around you. We're going to be competitive in the mornings now.' " Seeing the world through a window, Phyllis understood that her decision had to be based on more than her own ability to rise to a career opportunity; it had to rest on the genuine needs and the sincere support of others. Thus, she was prepared to face her potential loss, which occurred when *The CBS Morning News* did not rise high enough in the ratings.

Though her first risk might not have been the success for which she had hoped, her second risk was a triumph. It began with her positive loss: the recognition, the adult admission, that her efforts would not be enough to save the show. This was followed by the practical loss of the show itself. The worst potential losses — the possibility of rejection, regret, an empty future — did not occur. Instead, Phyllis said with conviction, "I'm glad I took the risk. And I'm glad I walked away. I know now I'm stronger for having done both. I learned if you don't take a risk, you don't grow. If you don't grow, you can't be satisfied. If you're not satisfied, you can't be happy. You have the right to be happy. . . . That doesn't mean the whole episode wasn't difficult, but the experience has strengthened me. I'd feel different, of course, if I had hurt someone else, but I was the only one hurt. Perhaps the greatest lesson in this for me, and maybe for others, is that a risk doesn't have to succeed to be valuable. You grow stronger even when risks don't work out. How sad I would be today if I had not tried. It was a great opportunity."

Phyllis's winning the Miss America crown was a victory of romantic dimensions, but no more constructive than the risk that concluded with the insight *You grow stronger even when risks don't work out.* Irving Wallace too had fulfilled himself, had realized his risk, irrelevant of his prosperity, even before a single novel had been sold, when he recognized that "I have to live with myself and be free to say the things I want to say." Thus, he could later conclude, "I knew that the writing of *The Man* was my real success. I had kept my word."

Like Irving and Phyllis and Carol Burnett, Gloria Steinem, Jim Webb, Hugh Downs, and the many others whose lives we are examining, we cannot perceive risks as the adults we hope to be until we erase the silver reflection — until, like the extraordinary woman we're about to meet, we find interests outside ourselves to which we can devote ourselves.

I stepped into the lobby of the Grand Hyatt Hotel in Manhattan to meet Mimi Silbert. Barely five feet tall, she stood quietly near a pillar, unnoticed, as travelers bustled past. I knew there had been scores of newspaper and magazine articles about her, dozens of radio and television interviews with her, and her career had been profiled on *This Is Your Life.* Yet who would suspect, I thought, that the slight, sandy-haired woman in the white linen jacket and black skirt was in fact one of the most dynamic, successful, and sensitive crusaders in America?

For seventeen years, Mimi, who is forty-five, has been the leader of the renowned Delancey Street Foundation, a residential treatment center for former drug abusers, prostitutes, and convicts — transformed human beings who in one moment may be doing business with major corporations such as the Bank of America and in the next may be selling Christmas trees on vacant lots. The Delancey Steet Foundation, which Mimi joined shortly after it was begun, runs without government aid; it is entirely self-supporting. The people who stay earn their way. Its eight hundred residents live in mansions in San Francisco and in some of the best neighborhoods in Los Angeles, New Mexico, North Carolina, and Brewster, New York. More than three thousand people have "graduated" from Delancey, which Dr. Karl Menninger described as "the best and most successful rehabilitation program I have studied in the world." Some of them are now attorneys and police officers, teachers and corporate executives.

The program is direct and strict. Most residents have been convicted of various crimes, many violent ones, and they arrive as functional illiterates. To graduate, each resident must earn a high school equivalency diploma and learn at least three marketable skills — a challenge that three out of four complete in an average of four years. More, they learn to talk, walk, and dress like sophisticated human beings.

This project is real — and at its center is Mimi, who earned a doctorate in criminology at the University of California at Berkeley. Her voice pops and splinters, its energy contagious, when she speaks.

"*What* are we going to talk about?" she asked me.

"You!" I said.

"That's boring," she replied — and I knew she'd be wrong.

In a few minutes we were sitting in Trumpets, a restaurant in the Hyatt, and I asked Mimi to describe the residents of Delancey Street.

"The people we take in," she said, "have hit bottom in their lives. Many have been drug addicts. Almost all have been poor, really poor, trapped outside what we normally consider the American system. They've ended up on the receiving end of life — receiving welfare, but not enough to live decently; receiving therapy, but not enough to help. The only thing they've received in large doses is punishment; they've served an average of four terms each in prison. Usually they've lived with great violence in their lives, and they're illiterate, with no discernible job skills. Six months is about as long as most of them have held any job. Work attitudes and work ethics thus are nonexistent among them. By the time they walk through our doors, they're bitter, angry, and cynical. They believe they are nobodies. Their frustration has showed itself in a vicious hatred of society, second only to the hatred they have for themselves. They have incredible energy — but it's directed negatively.

"Delancey Street is a boarding school, as I see it, like Andover or Exeter. The average stay is four years, just like at Harvard. The idea is to teach our residents all they need to know to live legitimately and successfully, to contribute and to participate in society. They're taught vocational skills, academic skills, art appreciation. They attend operas, learn to read fancy and complex restaurant menus, read great literature. We teach them how to set a table and how to choose and wear clothes properly. Now, not everyone will love the opera, but if someone is going to dislike it, he's going to dislike it because he has experienced it, not because it's something *other* people do. We teach money management and how to read contracts.

"Mainly, though —" Mimi's voice suddenly deepened, and she emphasized each word "— we teach how to believe and how to love. This takes unbelievable courage on the part of our residents. They are desperately afraid. To believe in caring and closeness, to trust, is difficult for people who have hurt others and who have been burned all their lives. Finally — and it takes a long time — a leap of faith is required. It's believing a declaration: *I can be decent.* I can care and I can show it and I can get close to people and not hurt them, not destroy them or me. This integrity and sensitivity is so difficult to learn, and it's precisely what they want to learn, even when they most pretend that they do not care. When they shout loudest, it's to cover an almost childlike desire for people to be good to them and to be good themselves.

"This is what we spend a lot of time on — caring. The way the place is structured, they *have* to care, because there's no staff, only me. They have to care for each other, or they will die. The horror of Delancey Street is that when people split, leave early, don't make it for one reason or another, they're soon dead. Literally, we fight for lives. We have success because we believe in something larger than ourselves; we plan all the time, talk incessantly about how we need to prepare for the kids now standing on street corners, kids we don't know but who are going to need help. We build not for ourselves but for them, for the future."

"What was your vision seventeen years ago?"

"I could imagine a place where each person had dignity, where all lives mattered. I've focused my life on people who are really poor, those who don't believe they can make it, who have convinced themselves that they are either crazy or evil. They see themselves — usually accurately — as castoffs and castouts, at the bottom of the heap, society's garbage."

"Is your vision different today?"

"My vision today is bigger and more burning, because it has been fueled. I started out blindly idealistic and have come face to face with the horrible realities of injustice and disappointment. When I began, I romanticized the poor; I suspected that the poor were somehow better, more real, than the rich, that they cared more about the things that really matter, that they were more loyal to each other. After seventeen years, I understand that the poor often have led terrible lives, that they can be nasty without discriminating about whom they're nasty to, including me. I did not anticipate how vicious human beings could be. Nor did I grasp that I might be the only person who believed in them. What happens, though, is that sometimes I can see a spark in their eyes, a tiny little light, barely visible. In that light, which ignites an inferno in me, I envision the future; I see these same people in a couple of years as decent, productive people."

"How were you treated at the start?"

"At night we'd have group sessions, and I'd be verbally assaulted by the participants on behalf of every professional that they had ever come in contact with. They'd shriek at me, 'What the hell do *you* know? You never shot dope. You've never been locked up. You damn pinko broad, who the hell are you to come here and tell us anything?' I took the abuse personally, and I was deeply hurt. I'd listen, then say softly, 'I can't believe you guys feel this way.' I'd desperately try not to cry. I'd hold it in, and at the end of every group session, I'd walk around the block with tears rolling from my eyes.

"Two guys were particularly mean, Abe and Nate. One was a huge Hispanic, the other a huge black. Both had false teeth. I remember this clearly because they'd yell at me with such intensity, such brutal rage, sometimes their teeth would come flying at me across the room, streaming spittle. I felt very small and very much alone. The poor, as I said, were not the romantic folk I'd imagined. Nevertheless, I would be conciliatory: 'I'm sorry,' I'd say, 'for making you this angry. I did not intend to provoke you. I intended only to . . .' No matter what I said, they'd ridicule me further. They'd shout, 'How dare you pretend to care! We're going through this bullshit with you for *nothing*. It's not going to work, anyway!'

"Until then, I had thought if I did good — this is not pleasant to recall, Walter — people would recognize how terrific I was and would respond: 'God, what a wonderful person Mimi is.' Instead I was vilified. It hurt terribly. I didn't understand. *Poor* Mimi." She paused, laughing. "*No one* seemed to understand that I was wonderful. Then one day I snapped, and I told the truth."

"What exactly did you say?"

"*Exactly?*"

I nodded.

"I let loose. In utter fury, I screamed, 'Who the hell do you think you're talking to? You're damn right I haven't shot dope and I haven't served time in prison — and that's good. You already know how to do that. You're here to learn something else, how to make it in life. *That* I can teach you, because unlike you, I *have* made it. I *am* a success. If you stopped acting like such self-destructive jerks and listened to me instead, if you did what I suggested, maybe you'd end up being somebody. Now I'm sick of *your* bullshit!' "

"What happened?"

"Instant silence — and respect. I had been straight; I had stood up for myself. In time I grew very close to both men. I trained them, and I yelled at every mistake they made. I took them under my wing twenty-four hours a day. Today Abe is the vice president of Delancey Street."

"What is Abe like?"

"Back then he was slimy and violent, an angry man who had been locked up since childhood — who had, in fact, been an inmate of every prison in the state of California, including the youth facilities. He had been an addict since he was twelve, and he was a member of a gang called the Mexican Mafia, a group sworn to kill. Simply, at the time, he was slick, mean, and incredibly violent. Today Abe is one of the most brilliant and sensitive counselors to be found anywhere."

"When did it turn for Abe?"

"I can't recall the day or moment, but I remember vividly when *he* recognized how different he'd become. He'd been with Delancey Street for five years, and I trusted him completely. Thus, when the California state legislature asked me to examine the prison system, I hired Abe as an assistant and had him accompany me to San Quentin, one of the prisons in which he had been incarcerated. I knew I'd be interviewing gang leaders in what's called lock-down, an isolated section. Abe would be an asset, I thought, because I was sure that the gang leaders would see me initially as a little white social worker — you know the kind, precisely what I was when I started at Delancey Street. I could cut through that on my own, but having Abe with me, I felt, would speed the process. Midway through the interview with the head of the Mexican Mafia, though, Abe excused himself to go to the bathroom — and he didn't return."

"What happened to him?"

"After the interview I found him, and he was pale as a sheet. 'What's the matter?' I asked him.

" 'My stomach,' he said. 'I've been vomiting in the bathroom.'

"We completed the rest of the interviews, though he looked terrible. Then, as we were leaving, with doors and gates clanking shut one by one behind us, a guard spotted Abe. 'Hey,' he said, 'I recognize you. You were here!'

" 'That's right,' Abe told him, smiling, 'and you're *still* here.'

"When we got to the car, Abe broke into tears. He sobbed and sobbed.

" 'I am not *that* anymore,' he said, 'absolutely not that. I looked at those guys. I know I would have given my life for them! Just to be accepted by them, I would have laid down my life. Don't you see, Mimi? Those guys are everything I would have been if you hadn't put up with my crap, if you hadn't believed in me. You believed in me!' He talked and talked, and we sat in that car parked on a dirt road near San Quentin for three hours. Abe cried the entire time. At first I wanted to say, 'Of course you're not that.' But somehow, thank God, I realized that the understanding had to come from within him, not from me. Abe had to see the truth with his own eyes. And he did — and he made me see it, and more."

"More?"

"More! He made me realize that the fight I had taken on was winnable, that the people I worked with, people who had given up on themselves as dead people, as the living dead, could change, could learn to believe in themselves. I was moved — and it was then that it all turned for me too. I could never go back. I knew I had to help. And then I cried too."

Mimi stood, took a deep breath, and said, "I feel that moment even as I talk about it."

When she sat down again, I asked: "There have been many more successes since that afternoon, haven't there?"

"Yes," she said.

"And more losses?"

"Yes, those too."

"What happened to Nate?"

"After my explosion," she began, "Nate too became sweeter. He was a very tough, very violent man who was illiterate, and consequently he was very sensitive about being thought of as stupid. He was well known among prison people, and he had a fearsome reputation. One day I asked him to break through for me, to go to school, to set an example for the others. Finally he agreed, and eventually he even called anyone who wouldn't

attend a chicken. He started to make it, but then his relationship with a woman in San Francisco failed and he wrote himself
off. 'I'm no good,' he told me. 'Don't believe in me. I'm no
good and I'll never be any good.'

"That's a big problem we have with the people of Delancey
Street. They don't believe that they can fix anything. When
they make a mistake, they believe they've blown it all. That's
it; they surrender; it's over. Nate quit —" she took another
deep breath "— and now he's back in prison.

"This is the reality we live with, how we define the world
by our choices. I am continually telling people who walk
through our doors that Delancey Street can't change the world;
rather, *only you can change you.* Every day, I tell our people,
you will have to make choices. Many will be right, and some
will be wrong. We all make mistakes. Thus, the second choice
you make is even more critical than the first: what you do when
you mess up."

"Like Nate?"

"Yes," she said. "There's still hope. Maybe when he's released
from prison —"

"When," I interrupted, "is it hopeless?"

She paused.

"Walter," she said, "the most horrible feeling is to love someone a lot, watch him become self-destructive, try to stop him
or give him the tools to stop himself, yet somehow not matter
enough. What I hate most is knowing there's nothing I can
do, that loss or failure is complete. At Delancey Street we had
a forty-seven-year-old man named Robert who had been the
son of a police officer. For thirty years he was an addict — and
twenty of those were spent in prison. He was torn between
the new feelings of warmth, caring, and being vulnerable, for
which he had a special gift, and a lifelong goal he had set in
prison: 'having the feel of money in my pockets.'

"He was with us for two years. We became very close. I believed he had a true talent for giving, and I knew he could do a lot for kids. But he left Delancey Street early to chase after that money.

" 'I'm using heroin again,' he told me over the telephone. 'I just needed a handle to grab onto. I know I've let you down.'

"He cried and asked if he could visit us, to regain his values and his strength — but twenty-four hours before he was to stop by, he overdosed on heroin. He was dead, and I felt like such a failure — so powerless, so hurt, so angry, so betrayed."

"When else do you doubt yourself?"

"Sometimes when I have to enforce the rules," she said. "We have three that are absolute: One, no drugs or alcohol. Two, no violence. Three, no threats of violence. In seventeen years no one has broken the violence rule, but fifteen people have broken the threat rule. I asked all of them to leave, with no exception. Some pleaded to stay. I remember one man in particular:

" 'Please,' he begged me, 'give me another chance.'

" 'No,' I told him.

"He dropped to the floor, grabbed my ankle, and he cried, 'Please, please, just one more chance.'

" 'No,' I told him again.

"I always advise our people not to focus their energy on the person who quits but to give their feelings to those who are still here, still struggling, still needing help. But the truth is, when I have to ask someone to leave, I end up locking myself in the bathroom and crying my eyes out. I'm the only person who can throw a resident out of Delancey Street. It's a large, lonely responsibility —"

She paused.

"— so I become filled with self-doubt, questioning whether I should have made an exception, as in the situation I just described. After all, I'll argue with myself, it's only a rule.

"I can't kid myself, though. We have gang members who have sworn to kill each other. Few people at Delancey Street have not experienced the most extreme forms of violence. I'm certainly not large enough physically to control our people. Also, it would be easy for those who've led hard lives to mistake niceness for weakness. I have to rely on my willingness to enforce the rules — on the strength of my personality. I know I can never allow a violent atmosphere to develop, and that begins with threats. I can't bend. That said, in my heart I'm still not sure whether my problem is that I should be tougher-gutted or that I have hardened too much."

"Mimi," I asked, "do the people of Delancey Street learn to take risks?"

"Absolutely," she said. "That's what Delancey Street is all about. Although some of their crimes may seem to involve great risk-taking or physical courage, that's a mirage. The facts are that these people, no matter how tough they may seem on the surface, are among the most frightened human beings on earth. It takes raw courage to survive Delancey Street, because they have to confront themselves. There's no running away. We teach them how to take risks, real risks, the largest of which are intimacy, trusting, sharing, and giving."

"What is it that you teach?"

"How to overcome the can'ts and the don'ts: I *can't* do this; I *don't* want that anyway. What we really mean when we say such things is that we have difficulty letting go of what's comfortable. How many human beings anywhere, not just at Delancey Street, hold onto a relationship merely because it exists? This fear of loneliness, abandonment, or failure can, if we let it, hold any of us back from doing exactly what each of us needs to do to feel fulfilled, which is to take a risk."

"How do you teach?"

"First, by role models. People who take risks are visible at Delancey Street. Others want to be like them. Second — well, I cheat. Because I know how hard it is to learn to take risks at first, I encourage the people here to help others take risks. Let me give you an example. One fellow who joined us after twenty years in prison could neither read nor write. After several months, he came to me.

" 'Mimi,' he said, 'this is great, but it's not for me.'

" 'I understand,' I told him. 'I can't beg you to change. Before you go, though, there's one thing you can do for me. A kid here, Tommy, worships you. He sees you as a hero, the best pickpocket in the world. He's only twenty years old. I don't want to see him spend a lot of time in the places you have, in prison. So before you go, help me with him.'

" 'Why should I help him? Nobody ever helped me!'

" '*We* did! If you want to leave, *leave* — but first help someone, because we tried to help you.'

"He took Tommy under his wing, but to tutor him, he had to learn to read, which he did. Also, of course, he had to tell Tommy the truth about prison and his career. 'You ain't tough because you survive in prison,' he said. 'You're just dead. What you can't admit in the joint is that what you really want to do is wake up, look in the mirror, and see yourself as a man.'

"In time, both made it." Mimi paused again. "You know what the secret to Delancey Street is?"

"What is that?"

"These folks want what every human being desires: They want to be somebody. Simply to admit that takes guts. What's different about Delancey Street residents is that they've hit bottom. If they fail to take the risks the world presents, they die. Maybe they have an advantage in that they *know* what will happen if they don't take risks. It may be easier for the rest of us to fool ourselves."

"Mimi," I said, having saved for last the question I most wanted to ask, "why do you do this?"

"I touch someone. I see lives change. I live with great joy. How can I explain what it feels like to help a person, to look into that person's eyes and see what she or he can be? I feel love and triumph, and . . ."

"And?"

"*I* want to be somebody."

The key to successful risk-takers like Mimi is their solid core, the strength of their convictions. It's why the pilot of Delancey Street can survive, even though there are times when, as she says, "I end up locking myself in the bathroom and crying my eyes out. . . . I become filled with self-doubt."

Successful risk-takers wipe away the silver.

Liz Smith recalled, "I was extremely involved with love and romance when I was younger, and I rushed like a mad person trying to resolve my conflicts — but now I think the greatest thing that has happened to me is the wonderful friends I've made along the way. They are people I can really count on. This is the love that's really important. I had to be older, to have lived my life, to come to this truth."

Most of the great human beings I have known, who include Liz and Mimi, inwardly war with themselves. What distinguishes these leaders is not necessarily some inner peace, but rather how they've learned to organize their lives around a noble motive and to focus on it. *They see outside themselves* — an observation I was reminded of a few days after my dinner with Mimi, when I returned to the same hotel, this time to meet with another lively leader, one of the most respected managers in baseball.

*

Through the tall windows of the Grand Hyatt's Crystal Fountain restaurant I could see the Chanin Building across Forty-Second Street and when I stretched, I could just spot a patch of bright blue sky above. How appropriate, I thought, because my breakfast companion could be described as blue — *Dodger* blue, to be precise. He was Tommy Lasorda.

As he made his way to our table, several people hailed him, and at every greeting he smiled cordially and waved back. Tommy had led the Dodgers for eleven seasons, and on this summer morning in 1987 I couldn't resist asking, "Are you going to beat my Mets tonight?"

"We're sure going to try," he told me. "We have the players to do it."

At fifty-nine, he had hair as white as his cotton shirt; his tie was blue, of course, as were his sports jacket and his eyes — those penetrating, lively, smiling eyes. Even sitting, he expressed energy. He was, I knew, a tough man. He had not been gifted with great talent; he had not been a sensational ballplayer. Rather, it was his tenacity, his drive to win, that had earned him a chance as a player in the major leagues when he was younger. And he had never left. His feelings about the Dodgers — *the* team, he'd say — had become sports legend. If there were a Dodger, Tommy Lasorda was that Dodger. As he said, he bled blue. He may have been only an average player, but as a manager he was exceptional. He had shown himself to be a brilliant tactician, a motivator. He *inspired*; he was a winner. How, I wondered, did he handle losing?

"Tommy, what do you tell your players when they lose?"

"I try to put a positive thought in their minds: 'That one's over — and today is the first day of a good winning streak,' " he replied. "The important thing for me to do when we lose is to encourage the players to focus on positive thoughts. Otherwise they'll think negative, which is destructive."

"How do you help young ballplayers learn to face risks?"

"You have to understand, Walter. Most athletes have a great fear of failing . . . Wait! I really want to explain this."

He sat back in his chair, then leaned forward again.

"Pressure!" he began again, gesturing. "That's the word I've been looking for. I think most talk about pressure is hogwash. The truth is, pressure comes from the inside, not from the outside, and I think it stems from the fear of failing.

"Let me give you an illustration of what I mean. Say we're playing the Yankees in the seventh game of the World Series. We're winning three-to-two in the bottom of the ninth inning, and they have the bases loaded, two outs. Dave Winfield is their hitter. How's that? Well, if we've all done our jobs right, every player has been taught to say to himself before the pitcher throws the ball, 'I want that ball hit to *me!* I'm going to react just as I've learned to, just as I've practiced it a thousand times. Come on, *please* hit it to me!' Now what if instead a player says to himself, 'Geez, if it's hit to me and I miss it, we'll lose the game.' What's he really doing? He is creating pressure, because he's thinking about failing. You see, only when the player thinks positive can he deal with his fear of failing. So that's why I try to keep a positive attitude in the players' minds at all times.

"Look, I'm no different from anyone else. I get tired, dejected, depressed. But no matter what I feel, when I walk into that ballpark, I have to wear a winning face, because winning, happiness, drive, determination are contagious. If you hang around whiners and complainers — people focused on failing — it won't be long before you'll want to jump off the building with them. *We're all players in this game.* A father comes home after a bad day, and his head's hanging down. He's sullen, can't be bothered. What's the atmosphere in the house? Does he make it easier or more difficult for his family? And what about *him?* Is he happy now that he's made everyone else unhappy? The next day's a good one, so he brings home a smile. What's the atmosphere now?

"Walter, these are choices we make. I'm not trying to say that real tragedy doesn't occur in our lives, or that we should ignore it or pretend it doesn't happen. No, not at all. What I'm suggesting is that more often than we may realize, we *choose* whether we're happy or not."

"How important do you feel you are to the Dodgers?"

"I've never gotten a base hit for this team. I've never hit a home run. I've never struck anyone out. Yet I've been manager of the year three times, and I've managed in three World Series, and I've managed in three All-Star games. Now, whatever success I've achieved as a manager is a reality only because of the contributions of my players. I need them; they don't need me. If I got so sick tonight that I couldn't show up at the ballpark, the game would be played without me. But if my players were so sick that *they* couldn't show up, there would be no game. Fans come to see players, not managers, perform. When managers or coaches of athletic teams begin to think *they're* the ones who win the games, they're naive. And something else."

"Yes?"

"When someone is wrapped up in his own self-importance, he always makes a small package, doesn't he? I think we have to believe in and be moved by principles larger than ourselves. In the end, I believe that's the only way we find either real self-worth or happiness. For me, it's a love of my family and of my God and of my great country and —"

"Dodger *blue!*" I interrupted.

"Yes," he said, "of course."

Tommy reminds us, "Pressure comes from the inside, not from the outside, and I think it stems from the fear of failing."

True, isn't it?

To diminish the pressure we place on ourselves when facing real risks, we have to understand what a baseball player must grasp:

I am responsible for what I feel.

More, we need to recognize that the natural anxiety that rises within any normal human being when faced with an important choice will be positively directed, as Tommy suggests, only when we first do something basic — even *before* we decide whether we're seeing the risk as a child, as an adolescent, or as an adult. We must take a step that's so obvious it is often overlooked:

Set a *clear* goal.

We cannot succeed if we stumble here. Without a clear goal, we cannot know our progress in a risk — or even be sure when to quit.

Jim Webb described his feelings of desperation when he realized that "my dad had been a career serviceman — and I had no other goal but to serve." And Gloria Steinem recollected her painful earlier years: "I ran from my childhood, the poverty and the humiliation. I had no goals."

Olivia de Havilland, Hugh Downs, Mimi Silbert, and Liz Smith had goals, and when I asked Carol Burnett what she was most afraid of, she replied: "To wake up one morning and discover that I have no goal. *That* would be frightening."

W. Clement Stone observed that people *can* learn to take risks, "but they must have a goal."

According to Roger Smith, "Once an objective is clear — and we should not proceed unless it *is* clear — we need to set reasonable goals to achieve that objective."

Phyllis George had the objective, which she exceeded, of making the top ten in the Miss America contest, and she made her goal clear again with *The CBS Morning News.*

Joyce Brothers recalled her decision to go for the $64,000

question: "Once I realized — admitted to myself — my new objective, the risks really grew."

Now remember Robert, the forty-seven-year-old addict who died of a drug overdose, who envisioned only "having the feel of money in my pockets."

When I joined the Marines, I was making a plea similar to Robert's: *I want to be somebody*. I didn't set a clear goal, though, until I became a student at the Marine Corps base in San Diego — an effort that ultimately led to a promotion. Decades later I again had to evaluate a career choice, only this time I received an opportunity almost too good to be true.

It was six o'clock on a Monday morning during the spring of 1980, and I was lying in bed, my eyes wide.

"Did you sleep?" my wife asked.

"Not so well," I replied.

"What did you decide?"

"Can you guess?" I asked.

"This time," she told me, shaking her head, "I don't have the slightest idea."

"Good," I said, "because until a few minutes ago, I didn't know myself."

I was the managing editor of *Parade*. Through the efforts of the executive recruiting firm Heidrick and Struggles, I had been asked if I'd like to become president and chief executive officer of a large company, an offer that included a salary far higher than the one I was earning at *Parade*.

"That's very generous," I told the chairman of the board, "and I'd like to take a few days to think about it. If it's okay with you, I'll give you my answer on Monday."

"That's fine," he said.

"One other thing," I added. "I'd like to speak to all of the directors of the company."

"That's fine, too," he replied.

When I spoke with each of the five, I asked "Why did you choose me?"

The company was experiencing what they called "a period of transition," and all agreed that the corporation needed what they described to me as a strong, innovative leader. Three of the five cited my prior experience as a general manager in the Gannett Company as a major factor. None noted that I was an editor.

The publisher of *Parade*, Carlo Vittorini, who learned about the offer in a telephone call from one of the directors, argued vigorously against the opportunity. After a lengthy discussion, he left for a vacation in Hawaii, where he wrote a note to me that restated his view and concluded, "I want you to stay with *Parade*!"

I was moved by Carlo's support, but I also recognized that he was an interested observer; whatever decision I made would have some impact, if only a minor one, on his magazine. Since my Gannett experience was a factor, I decided to call the man who led Gannett — its chairman, Allen H. Neuharth, whom I had known for several years.

"Walter," he told me, "I think you should decline."

"Why?"

"First off, I think you can probably fix their company a hell of a lot faster than they think you can — but what are you going to do then? You should not be out there solving someone else's problems; you should edit a magazine. I'd like to see you stay at *Parade*. I'm sure the Newhouse family, the people who own *Parade*, recognize your talent. But even if they don't, the thing you have to keep in mind is not only what you do, but *why* you do it. You're thirty-five. Let me put that in perspective. I think when people are in their twenties, they're just growing up, and it's not altogether crucial what they do. In their thirties they begin to prepare, to try to find out what they *really* want to do, which is what they do in their forties. I can't believe being the chief executive officer of this company, however good the money and benefits may look to you now, is how you see yourself at forty. Walter, I can only tell you what I believe. I know the salary and the perquisites are attractive. It's a tough decision. But I hope you say no."

The money *was* attractive. I asked myself, what is the risk? Failure, perhaps. No, I thought. I knew that as much as I would not like to admit it, if I managed the company to the best of my ability and it soured, I could handle a failure. After all, I had failed before.

What would I lose?

"The thing you have to keep in mind," Al had advised, "is not only what you do, but *why* you do it."

At about three o'clock on Monday morning, a few hours before I had to give my decision, I sat up in bed and remembered another night twenty years earlier, when I was a teenager, lonely and driven, pounding on an old Remington portable typewriter. Secretly, more than anything else, I had wanted to be a writer, and for several months I had surreptitiously worked on a novel. One Sunday, shortly before 10:00 P.M., I typed the last sentence, and I was joyous. The ending had been especially difficult for me, because when I had started to write the book I had thought it would conclude happily. As I labored night after night, though, I discovered that this particular story, to be true, had to be a tragedy; it was about an interracial romance that ends in separation.

I titled the short novel *Hanover Hill* and gave the manuscript to my mother, who, not surprisingly, loved every word and cried at the ending. Thus encouraged, I packaged *Hanover Hill* the following week, walked to the post office a few blocks away, and, at fifteen years old, mailed my book to a publishing company that sold novels. Then I waited. And waited.

Finally, after about two months, I received a package from the publisher. It was the same size as the manuscript I had mailed. I trembled as I held it. This is it, I thought. They're going to publish my novel.

I tore the wrapping. It *was* my novel, and enclosed with it was a form letter advising me that *Hanover Hill* had been rejected.

My eyes filled as I placed the manuscript back in its wrapper. I carried the little package through the back door, down the fire escape, to the enclosed garbage shed behind our tenement. When I found a can only half filled, I tossed my novel onto a filthy, torn brown paper bag.

Two decades later, wide awake in the night, I could still feel regret — not that I had written *Hanover Hill*, but that I had thrown it away. It was then, the desire of that teenager alive in my mind, that I understood finally the risk I was facing. I had accepted my positive loss, which was the recognition that I needed to stretch in my career. However, when it came to the practical loss I had to take, I was, I realized, standing on the wrong drawbridge; it would be wrong for me, at least at this stage of my life, to give up writing and editing. If I take this job, I told myself, it's for the money alone. Al was right: "The thing you have to keep in mind is not only what you do, but *why* you do it." The truth told, it was too easy for me to dismiss the potential losses, particularly failure.

"No," I told the executive recruiter at Heidrick and Struggles, "this is not for me."

Later that same year I was promoted from managing editor to editor of *Parade* magazine — but like Irving Wallace, I know in retrospect that I was fulfilled earlier, that night when I began to realize my clear goals: I want to write, to edit, to speak, to communicate as well as I am able; to try to affect the world around me positively and to encourage others to do the same. Why I feel so strongly, I'm not sure. But this belief, I know today, is who I am — and though I'm convinced that no one moment defines any of us, I started to find myself in the risk I declined.

The path to rejecting a risk, as I did, is the same route we take to say yes:

Define a clear goal.

Review the positive, practical, and potential losses.

Determine whether the risk is one of trust, of identity, or of something larger. How we perceive the risk — whether we respond as a child, as an adolescent, as an adult — is critical. How might I have seen the opportunity presented to me by Heidrick and Struggles if I had thought like a child or an adolescent? I suspect I would have said yes.

Decide — but before you do, let's review the advice of a fellow who has taken many risks, from conquering his fear of water to being co-host of *20/20*: "If we start by taking small risks first," advises Hugh Downs, "we're encouraged to take larger risks — and if we know clearly what's at stake, we can take risks more wisely. For example, if I was asked whether I'd drive a car at one hundred and twenty-five miles per hour on Route 101, I'd have to reply yes and no! Just to drive it, I'd say no. The risk's too great. However, if I was told that my child was down the highway, in serious trouble, urgently needing my help, I'd say yes. And of course, to give ourselves the best chance for success with any risk, we must prepare well. . . . I must prepare as if my life depends on it — because after all, it does."

Few people I know understand the value of preparing for life as well as a gentle friend of mine who saw a great many die.

*

One winter evening, after I had met Elie Wiesel for the first time, I wrote a note to myself: "If ever eyes revealed a soul, they would be his — *dark* brown eyes, the most distinctive and compelling of any human being I have known." Now, several years later, as we sat together for lunch at the Marco Polo restaurant in the Waldorf-Astoria during a bright, sunny September afternoon in 1987, his eyes again struck me. Few photographs, I marveled, capture the depth of his eyes, their sadness, the opaque reflections of the unimaginable tragedy he has witnessed. I remembered, as I studied this slender man sitting across from me with wispy and disheveled gray hair and a modest — no, *humble* — demeanor, that when the Nobel committee recognized him with the 1986 Nobel Prize for Peace, they called Elie Wiesel a messenger to mankind, one of earth's most important spiritual leaders. And they described his message as one of peace, atonement, and human dignity.

He was only fifteen in 1944, when the Nazis, in what may still have seemed to some of them an inexorable march to glory, finally arrived in his remote Carpathian Mountain hometown, the village of Sighet, Hungary. The soldiers, by then chillingly efficient at their murderous business, quickly deported the entire Jewish population. Elie's family first was sent to Auschwitz, where his mother and younger sister were killed, and then he and his father were ordered on to the Buchenwald camp, where his father was starved to death. Like Elie, his two older sisters survived.

When the Allies liberated Buchenwald in 1945, the young survivor vowed to himself not to speak for ten years about the horrors he had seen, and he kept this vow of silence. When finally he did speak, he was like a bursting dam. Starting in 1958 with the memoir called *Night*, he has written more than thirty books and hundreds of essays and articles, and given speeches, and they have, as he hoped, paid eloquent witness to the Holocaust. He has also spoken out for Southeast Asian refugees, South African blacks, the Miskito Indians of Nicaragua, Argentine political prisoners, and, in a passionate and historic work titled *The Jews of Silence*, Soviet Jewry.

This teacher and leader who has lived with such courage, who as an American citizen has received the Congressional Gold Medal, and as a citizen of the world has been honored with humanitarian and literary recognition from so many other nations — what, I wondered, did he fear?

"My greatest fear," he told me, "has been that what happened during the Holocaust will not be transmitted. I say this knowing that it is the most documented tragedy in history and that never before has such misery been so carefully recorded by so many — by the victims, the killers, the bystanders. The tormentors themselves kept statistics; they had competitions. Murder squads competed to see who killed more. Detailed records were meticulously kept, with boasting entries like 'Ten days — eighty thousand Jews.' Yet in spite of these documents, the books, the pictures, the films, all the testimony, the words of the survivors and the witnesses, still — *still* some things remain beyond comprehension."

"Elie," I asked, "how did *you* survive?"

"By accident. Every day ten thousand people left the camp. Most were killed; others died on the way. I happened to be in the group of two or three hundred at the gate who were the overflow; the quota was filled. It just happened. Not only could I not plan it, I did not want to plan it. I was a boy, and to remain alive without those I loved, those who loved me — well, it did not seem like life as I wanted it."

"Did you believe you were going to die there?"

"I was convinced I would not survive. I wasn't the type to survive. I was always a weak child. I was sickly, always going to doctors, only interested in study, not sports; always vulnerable."

"Did you take risks?"

"I was afraid to take risks. I was timid. I always obeyed. I never tried to obtain anything that was not given to me. I took one portion of soup, one portion of bread, never tried to 'organize' more."

"At sixteen you knew your parents had been killed, yet you ended up doing something positive out of that."

"It wasn't easy. It took many years."

"To overcome anger?"

"Overcome? No, I'm still angry. I am outraged. I am not against anger. I am against *hate*."

"Why don't you hate those responsible?"

"It would be silly to reduce such enormous horror, a tragedy unprecedented in the history of man, to hatred. That would be a betrayal of my parents and my friends —" he paused, then continued, speaking slowly "— because if I hated, I would betray their deaths. The enemy *wanted* us to hate him. I *refuse*. I will not grant the killer's wish. In the Bible, the first death is a murder. Cain is slaying his brother, Abel. Is the point of the murder that brothers ultimately must kill each other? Or does the story mean that whoever kills, kills his brother? We're told not to hate our brother in our hearts; hatred inevitably destroys the hater as well as the hated. The choice is ours. I choose to believe that he who kills, kills his brother, and finally himself. *We* are responsible for what we are.

"In 1945 I was among four hundred children who came to France. The youngest was six — he had been hidden by inmates at Buchenwald — and the oldest was seventeen. Some had survived four, five, even six years in camps in which brutality and death prevailed. Not one became a criminal. Most, in fact, chose philanthropic careers as teachers, doctors, patrons of the arts, social workers. Not one betrayed humanity. After the war, it would have seemed normal for survivors to return to Germany, Hungary, or Poland to avenge the deaths of their parents, their brothers and sisters, their friends. And there was no risk in doing that. We could have killed a Mengele or a Barbie — all of them — and we would not have been reproached, because in that year, 1945, the camps had been opened and the world was shocked. It would have seemed logical for the victims to kill their tormentors. More, it was a risk to allow them to live: Could the Nazis re-emerge? After all, having stolen billions of dollars' worth of jewels and other valuables from Jewish homes all over Europe, they had great wealth. It was risky for the victims to leave the tormentors alive; the tormentors still had their money, their contacts, their weapons hidden somewhere. Yet we did not kill — and I think we were right. The survivors did not allow the relationship between the victims and their tormentors to be reduced to a level of hatred."

"Was there hatred in the camps?"

"Yes. In Buchenwald I saw hate. The camp inside was ruled and managed by inmates, and anti-Semitism existed among them too — some Ukrainians and Poles hated Jews and allowed their frustration and rage to overcome them. I have seen inmates kill inmates. But also I have seen people take risks and remain human. I can tell you I have seen a man take bread and offer it to an unknown inmate. Yet it was dangerous not to eat one's own bread; that was one day less to live. I have seen a man intervene on behalf of someone else. This was not a father-son relationship; they were strangers. Tenderness existed even there among people.

"I remember one night during the last days of the war — it was April 5, 1945 — when the Americans were coming closer to Buchenwald, and suddenly the loudspeakers blared, 'All Jews out!' As we began to assemble, the camp police force, which was made up of Scandinavian students and resistance members, whispered to us, 'Don't go. Don't go. Run back and hide.'

So all of the children, including me, ran back and we hid.

"Forty years later I was in Israel attending a dinner in my honor. A Norwegian ambassador was asked to say a few words. 'I am so glad to meet Elie Wiesel again,' he began. When he spoke, I looked up, but I did not recognize him. Have we met? I wondered. Where? Then it came to me: *Buchenwald*.

"In my response I said, 'All these years I have looked to thank the person who saved my life and those of my friends. Thank you and the others,' I said, 'for sending us back to the barracks.' "

I gestured toward Elie's sleeve.

"Why," I asked, "did you not have the numbers the Nazis tattooed on your arm removed?"

"Walter, I am not ashamed of my tattoo. Again, I could not allow the enemy to govern the spirit of my life. That's why we who survive refuse to hate. The killer wanted us to hate, and he wanted us to be ashamed of our tattoos. I am not ashamed. Neither am I proud. Simply, I accept it. It is part of me now. *He* should be ashamed, not me."

"Why did you wait ten years before speaking about the Holocaust?"

"I really believe my survival had no meaning, but because I survived, I have to give it meaning. For ten years I was afraid to speak. I was afraid that what I wanted to say, I would not be able to say. Truly, the testimony that the survivors have to give cannot be given. The killer's brutality was so extreme as to deprive us of the language to tell of his brutality. The words, I feared, did not exist. That's why I waited ten years, to purify the language in me."

"Are you sure of the words today?"

"They are as close as possible to what I want to say."

"What's your greatest risk?"

"My greatest risk is to fail to be understood clearly. If a

witness tells his story and is misinterpreted or misunderstood, then no matter how good his intentions might be, he has become a false witness."

"How would you advise others to prepare for risks?"

"First we must understand that there can be no life without risk — and when our center is strong, everything else is secondary, even the risks. Thus, we best prepare by building our inner strength, by sound philosophy, by reaching out to others, by asking ourselves what matters most."

"What have *you* learned to value most?"

"I have learned, because of what I've witnessed, to sanctify life. I *cherish* life." He paused, seeming to weigh his words even more carefully. "And because I have seen so many children killed," he continued, "every child is precious to me. When I see a child, I cry inside. I have come to celebrate life, not only mine and yours, but the lives of people whom neither of us will ever come to know. We all work with what we are, Walter. I could have been crushed by events or saved by them."

He paused again.

"I *chose* to be a writer and a teacher. We cannot live for the ifs — if this happened, if that, if I had . . . Each of us can make a difference. Personal happiness cannot be solitary; it must involve someone else, be it a girlfriend or boyfriend, a husband or a wife or a child, a teacher, a student, a friend — *some* other person. We need each other."

"How can an average person make a difference in so large a world?"

"Very few people make history, but it is given to all of us to participate in history."

"How do we achieve this?" I asked.

"By taking history upon ourselves," he replied, his voice even, sure. "Consider, for example, the plight of the boat people in Indochina, human beings fleeing for their lives. A single citizen can help to open the door for a single refugee — or write a letter. By *participating*. If we do *something*, however small it may seem to be at first, we actively take part in history."

"Is this what you struggle toward?"

"Yes. For me, nothing is as evil as indifference. All parties suffer when an act of indifference occurs. A person who is being tortured can have hope, however frail, that perhaps somebody, someday, will learn of his torment and will cause it to stop. However, when a spectator enters the room, is seen by the tormented person, and does nothing, such indifference doubles, triples, quadruples the agony. Hope is lost; nothing is crueler. I believe the guilt of the bystander is at least as large as that of the tormentor. For me, indifference is the worst affliction troubling our society. All that I try to do — I don't do that much — is to fight indifference. A little bit here, a little bit there, hoping to break through to one person, then another."

"First we must understand that there can be no life without risk — and when our center is strong, everything else is secondary, even the risks. Thus, we best prepare by building our inner strength, by sound philosophy, by reaching out to others, by asking ourselves what matters most."

In the carefully chosen words of this eloquent man, we can hear the principles of Mimi Silbert, Olivia de Havilland, Roger Smith, Jim Webb, and others throughout these pages, including a minister who was once ridiculed.

As I sat in the Dutchess County, New York, office of Dr. Norman Vincent Peale, the author of one of this century's most inspiring and successful books, *The Power of Positive Thinking*, I considered how fortunate I was to be able to speak with a person whom I've admired all my life. It was a spring morning in 1987, and on that day he was eighty-nine, a *young* eighty-nine. One of the world's most famous ministers, he sat in a black leather executive chair behind his large walnut desk, folders and manuscripts in tidy little piles about him. He was nattily dressed in a dark blue wool suit, a blue and white striped shirt, and a maroon silk tie. His wife, Ruth, smartly attractive in a green suede suit and a pink blouse, sat near me and across from her husband.

I could feel his enthusiasm, so apparent in his demeanor, as clean and clear as a kitten leaning back about to spring, and it seemed to light those twinkling blue eyes. He was *ready*, and though he had published more than thirty books, had lectured around the globe, had moved millions, he was (and I shouldn't have been surprised) excited.

Because his classic work on positive thinking was one of a handful of books that had truly affected me, I felt that I knew Norman Vincent Peale. Meeting him confirmed that. I knew what I wanted to ask — and where to begin: "What is the greatest risk you have taken?"

"I was a minister in a working-class church in Rhode Island," he told me, "and I began to write books stressing that an individual, working within himself with the power of God, can gain victories in society, can right wrongs. This may not seem particularly provocative today, but at the time, a half century ago, this view made me anathema to large sections of the Protestant church, because it was a mixture of what my critics believed were competing beliefs. Teachers and ministers inveighed against my preaching, calling it Pealism. I had to ask myself, should I back down? I am not courageous at all, and the attacks against me were scathing. But I came to the conclusion that although I was afraid, I could not yield — and in the face of widespread ridicule, I took the biggest risk of my life: I kept preaching what I believed. The criticism grew, of course, and it was devastating. I was shaken more than once. Adlai Stevenson remarked at the height of it, 'Paul is appealing and Peale is appalling.' When we met years later, he took pains to explain to me that he had meant nothing harmful by his witty remark, and he asked, 'Did it bother you?' I assured him that it did not, but the truth is, it did. It bothered me a lot."

"What happened to your critics?"

"I have outlived them, for the most part. They're either dead or have softened. I'm not criticized so heatedly any longer, which leads me to believe that maybe I'm slipping." He chuckled.

"You're so self-assured," I said "You seem to know precisely who Norman Vincent Peale is. How does a person discover who he is?"

"A lot of people have trouble with that question — and I can understand why. When I was a young boy, I disliked myself. I was too short, too skinny. I thought I talked funny. I didn't even like my name, Norman Vincent. I remember the day when I was twelve that I screwed up my courage and marched into an Ohio courthouse and asked to see a judge.

" 'What can I do for you, Norman?' he asked me.

" 'I don't like my name,' I told him.

" 'What do you want your name to be?'

" 'William Howard,' I said, because William Howard Taft was president of the United States at the time, and I thought he was quite a guy.

" 'By the edict of this court,' the judge proclaimed, 'henceforth your name is William Howard.'

"I smiled.

" 'Are you happy now?' he asked.

" 'Yes,' I assured him, and I was — until I got home. My father was waiting, and he had heard from the judge.

" 'I am your father,' he told me, 'and I have the privilege of giving you a name. You are Norman Vincent Peale. Now take that name and make it mean something.' "

Dr. Peale paused, scratching his chin.

"Since that talk with my father," he said, "I've been who he said I was, but I realized recently that I might have been a little slower to fall into line than I remembered. Only the other day I happened to pick up an old childhood textbook of mine, and when I thumbed through it, I noticed it was signed William Howard Peale."

We both laughed.

He continued, now speaking more slowly, more forcefully.

"I've often thought it curious," he said, "how none of us has ever seen his face. When we look into a mirror, we see a reflection — but it's only a reflection, and the reflection's reversed and distorted. Yet if we *could* see our faces, would we know ourselves any better? I don't think so. We're not our skin cells, our hair cells, even our brain cells. We are what we believe, what we seek to achieve, what we love: *We are what we think.* After all, a heart is only muscle, and a brain is merely tissue. I believe that what goes on in someone's mind is who that person really is."

"Do you have an example?"

"Yes," he said. "I received a manuscript this morning from a woman who is horribly crippled. Nevertheless, she sees beauty all around her — in the birds, the changing leaves, in the moss on the forest floor. Truly, she lives in the world of her mind — and isn't it a beautiful world? Walter, when we impair our minds with hate or dishonesty or guilt, we can have no peace. Jesus taught that the way to life is to love. Hate, he told us, is corrosive, and love is expansive. This is a battle I've had to fight within myself, in my mind, all my life. I get angry and resentful and I have a mean streak —"

"*You?*" I interrupted.

"Yes, me. I was severely criticized when I wrote *The Power of Positive Thinking*, and as I said before, I felt hurt by it, and it made me angry. I had to remind myself every day of the love Jesus spoke of. Then I'd force myself to listen to the critics, to try to sift for the good in their observations. I learned when to fight back, which is when something we believe in is involved. And how to fight back, which is with love and not with hate."

"How do we do that?"

Norman looked toward Ruth, then back to me.

"The best way to find love," he said softly, "is to give love. People love those who love them. Recently I advised a lonely teenager that he should *beam* love — that without saying a word, he should beam love to his classmates, that before he sleeps at night, he should picture their faces and beam love again. A person who projects love will be loved all his life."

"Why didn't you give up under the criticism?"

"That's a good question. My father used to say that if you raise your head above the crowd, expect someone to try to slap it down. Now, that's a risky business, but when we stand up for something we sincerely believe in, I've found, we can take criticism, even grow from it."

"We can be ourselves?" I asked.

"Yes," he said. "I had this emphasized to me when, as a young minister, I was assigned to the University Methodist Church in Syracuse. It is a big, beautiful church with enormous Tiffany windows, and every Sunday its pews were filled with faculty and students of Syracuse University — an erudite, intellectual congregation. I prepared my sermons with great care, and I read them without dropping a line or missing a word. One particular professor at Syracuse, a talented speaker by the name of Hugh M. Tilrow, was widely respected at the time. One day he stopped by to see me.

" 'Norman,' he suggested, 'please don't try to preach a baccalaureate sermon every Sunday just because you think you have to, with professors and students in the pews. Now it's true that I am a professor, but I'm just a poor human being struggling for the joy of life. So when I sit in this church, you are my teacher.'

" 'What should I do?' I asked him.

" 'For a start,' he said, 'throw away your notes. Norman, stand there and speak from your heart and from your mind.'

" 'How about if I just carry my notes?'

" 'No, Norman, not even that. If you wanted to buy a car and the salesman started to read from a book, woul'd you have a lot of confidence in him?'

" 'Not a lot,' I agreed.

" 'Good,' he said. 'Don't even have those notes around. You don't need any crutches.'

" 'This is a big risk for me,' I told him. 'How will I remember what to say?'

" 'If you forget,' he advised me, 'just pray. What you can't remember, the Lord does not want you to remember. Norman, go up there and *tell us what you believe.*' "

"Did you follow the professor's advice?"

He nodded.

"I'll never forget the next Sunday. Alone, I walked up to that pulpit. No notes. I was so nervous. Well, I did it, and I've never used a note since. If I had not taken that risk — if I had not heeded the professor's criticism — I'd be a note-follower to this day. Funny, isn't it, how a single risk can so affect your life?"

I nodded.

"Norman," I said, "one of the most frequently asked questions I've heard is 'Why does God permit bad things to happen?' How would you answer?"

"If God can be said to have made a mistake," he began, "it was that when he created human beings, he thought they were wonderful. He gave them the right to choose. He gave them full freedom to choose — to be for him or against him, to be bright or to be dull. The reason people are hungry is not because God did not provide. Quite the contrary; the world's full of food and all else that human beings need. Hunger and poverty exist because we don't share, Walter. Some people grab off hunks; the strong prey on the weak. It is up to us, each one of us, to fix the system, to care for each other."

"And it's astounding," Ruth Peale continued the thought, with Norman nodding encouragement, "that man could create the intricacy of the atomic bomb, journey to the planets, but cannot seem to figure out how to distribute fairly the things mankind has learned to produce. Consider food. The technology exists to feed the world, but we do not. If we applied our minds and our hearts to this in a serious way —"

"— we could diminish hunger and poverty." Norman completed the sentence, his voice rising with enthusiasm. "And," he added, "we *should.*"

Elie Wiesel told us, "When our center is strong, everything else is secondary." Norman Vincent Peale now directs us to that center, to the fundamental question: Who am I? "We are what we believe," he suggests, "what we seek to achieve, what we love. *We are what we think.*"

This book, page by page, is about the necessary risks we face throughout our lives. We've reviewed goal-setting, losses, how we've come to perceive risks, and, with Elie Wiesel and Norman Vincent Peale, who we are. Two factors of consequence remain, though.

The first is timing. Here we are again on the drawbridge, but now we're small children, *very* small children, ill prepared to climb the incline ahead. We try, but we stumble, slip, roll back to the bottom. Similarly, in every critical life risk there is a moment too soon, a point at which we're not ready, either emotionally or substantially, to go forward. If we try, we fail.

Let's return to the drawbridge — this time, though, as strong, agile adults. We have the physical power to leap across, but, well, we decide we need to reconsider. Do we *really* want to reach the other side? Why today? Maybe we ought to learn more about this drawbridge. We linger. Suddenly we raise our eyes, and the gap is too great. Even if we were Olympic broad-jumpers, we'd plop into the drink. We've reached the moment too late; we've waited too long. If we try, we fail.

Timing isn't perfect for any risk; life's too unpredictable. Thus, the best — and the smartest — we can be is honest. When, we must ask, is the best time to take the risk? What will happen if we don't act then? Certainly, if we're as impulsive as we can be as adolescents, we increase our likelihood of failure, but more often than not, our concern over whether it's too soon is an excuse to live out the second example; we dawdle, find excuses *not* to act.

Back to the drawbridge. Again we're adults — and we know why we're here. We've studied the bridge and its movement, have a good sense of the widening gap, have a clear goal. At precisely the right moment, our hearts pumping, we dash ahead. Up the incline we go, growing stronger by the stride, our eyes now rising above the bridge's edge, glancing at the other side for the first time — how different it looks! — and we *freeze*, our feet cemented, our bodies falling, falling. We fail.

Often, as prepared as we might be, we understand our risks only when we take them. And if we're not prepared for *that*, we can freeze, as we did on the drawbridge, and we fail.

"I know that when I face risk, I have to make a commitment

at some point," Roger Smith said. "There comes a moment when reasoning and rational thought have been exhausted. Either I take the step, or I do not."

Frequently, as when Jim Webb left a secure future in the Environmental Protection Agency and Olivia de Havilland challenged the movie studios, the true weight of the decision is felt only in the doing. That was certainly true for me when I joined the Marines. How can we know what our boss will say about our resignation until we hand it to him? Neither can we know how a lover will respond until we actually risk saying goodbye. Risks are scary precisely because there *is* an unknown.

If we could predict with complete accuracy what would occur in a risk, we would feel no anxiety. We worry only because we care. We don't fret about what's meaningless to us. Thus, fear in mind, we come to another factor in risk-taking, courage. Consider the story of one man in a brutal world.

Andrew Vachss is a tough guy, a hard-talking attorney with a special practice, an attorney who also writes biting, graphic novels such as *Flood* and *Strega* — steamy, violent books about sudden death, brutalized children, sexual molestation, the dark side of human existence. As he sat across from me in a conference room a few steps from my Manhattan office, I wondered whether anyone knew the seamy world of deprivation better than this man. His practice is, as I said, special: Andrew defends children, *abused* children, and most of his cases are private, either criminal or civil. He lives on a daily basis with an ugliness that can be imagined by most people only in nightmares. The children he fights for may have been raped when they were a year old by their fathers or uncles, or tortured at age three. Some learn to murder from their mothers. A few, in their early teens, arrive every afternoon at the Port Authority

Bus Terminal from places like Minneapolis and Shreveport. However innocent they are when they step off the bus, within hours their bodies are for sale — if they survive that long.

These, and others, are the children of Andrew Vachss. At forty-four, he has served as an investigator for the U.S. Public Health Service, as a caseworker for the Department of Social Services, as director of a maximum-security juvenile institution. *New York* magazine described him as "an exception — a crusader and an expert, not in it for money." In addition to his private practice, Andrew Vachss works as a law guardian, appointed by the state to represent children — and he's unyielding, merciless, when separating and protecting the young from abusers. In and out of court, he's impatient; opposing attorneys, even some judges, have called him obnoxious — and worse.

He chain-smoked as we talked, and not surprisingly, his voice was hoarse. The collar of his blue and yellow striped shirt was open, and his black knit tie was loosely knotted. A black patch hung crookedly over his right eye, which was permanently damaged in an obscure alley when he was a child on the Lower West Side of New York. His curly black hair, like his personality, was unruly; his skin was tight, his flesh gaunt from the malaria he had caught in Biafra on a mission eighteen years earlier.

I had known Andrew for more than two years, though it seemed longer. I was sure he'd be candid.

"If you were asked to advise someone on how to take a risk," I asked, "what would you suggest?"

"I'm sure I'd ask him whether he knew what his net was."

"His net?"

"Yes, there's a big difference between being on a tightrope with a net and without a net. The trick is to reach into yourself to discover what your net is. Take you, for example. You take a lot of risks as an editor. Let's say one of them causes you to lose your job. You'd still be yourself, still have your family, your talent, your experience — your *net*. Also, you would know what you have at risk. No one should take a risk unless they truly understand what's at stake. Blindly leaping out of a window is not risk-taking. It's suicide, period. Risk implies a potential for gain and a potential for loss. The question is, what are you willing to lose? When kids ask me about fighting, I give them very simple rules: If you can take the worst possible result, then fight. If not, run."

"Have you ever thought of yourself as brave?"

"No, absolutely not. I'm not a brave person at all; I am a *careful* person."

"Do you love the children you help?"

"It would be hypocritical for me to say I love all of these kids. Some are so compelling you'd have to be subhuman not to love them. Others, because of what has been done to them, are not easily lovable; they have no love in them. Remember, we have to learn empathy. Essentially, a child is without self-control. He wants food, he takes it. He's angry, he cries. Not only must we teach the child self-control, but we must teach him to empathize, to feel the suffering of others, because the child feels only his own pain."

"Do all children learn to care?"

"No — and those who never learn to empathize are the most dangerous human beings on earth. They're ambulatory sociopaths, and they can be on Wall Street as well as in Attica prison. The classic is the kid raised in a multipathology home in which incest is only a part of the daily violence. Early on, the child turns predator; the victim becomes a victimizer. The challenge is to stop the child before he crosses that line, because it's as difficult, if not impossible, to rehabilitate a sixteen-year-old who preys on five-year-old children as it is to rehabilitate a thirty-five-year-old who preys on sixteen-year-old adolescents."

"Why do you take these cases?"

"The chance to affect some of these, the most deadly flowers human beings can produce — to affect those seeds — is important to me. Children, as I see it, are the only innocent things on the planet, and the rest is a judgment call. My chance to better the world is to help abused kids. If something's not done, or if it's done wrong, then we have tomorrow's Charles Manson."

"Does one child stand out?"

"There have been so many . . ." He stood, glanced out of the window down at Forty-Sixth Street, then turned back. "But there *was* one. I don't know if conventional people reading your book will understand."

"Please," I encouraged him.

"Some years ago," he began slowly, his voice softening, "I was placed in charge of a maximum-security institution, and in it I found this fourteen-year-old boy, a huge kid of about two hundred and fifty pounds, who had been beaten so badly so often that he had layers of scar tissue on his body and he was nearly anesthetized to pain. The state had removed him from his violently abusive home, but because he screamed and fought, the state locked him up, even though he had committed no crime. The prison kept him drugged with massive quantities of Thorazine and Stelazine. He was a pharmacological nightmare. He could control neither his bowels nor his bladder. He was a lump, a fearsome, frightening lump, because whenever he'd come out of this psychotropic haze, he'd attack anything that moved. Some of the places he had been in, kids had burned out cigarettes on his arms, used him as a stump. At one time or another, people had done everything cruel known to mankind to this boy. They said his IQ was in the forties.

"When I first met him, this drooling, terrifying blob out of

a Stephen King horror story, I looked dead into his eyes —
and I saw something. Now Walter, some people will say what
I saw was anthropomorphic, that I projected human qualities
into an animal. After all, I'm no psychiatrist; I had no training.
No matter. I knew in my heart what I saw. There was a human
being in there. I took a risk with his life — and with mine.
Without authorization, I ordered all medication stopped immediately.

"He turned into a lunatic. He was locked in a room, and
with the awesome strength of a crazy person, he wrecked the
place. He was totally out of control. I believed, despite this,
that I had a relationship with him. I entered the room. And
we fought. Had it been a fair fight, I would not have survived.
I was prepared, though. I hit him with blunt objects and a
chair. He broke two of my ribs.

"Finally I subdued him. Then something happened. As he
came to — I had knocked him out — he looked at me holding
my side and he spoke. 'What happened?' he asked. 'You broke
Andy's ribs,' an attendant said. Then that boy cried.

"That moved me and every other person in that institution.
It was fifteen years ago, but that moment is as vivid to me as
if it happened this morning. His name is Allen, and he still
comes to see me from time to time. No, he doesn't live a crime-
free life. If he's physically touched, he'll instantly assault. But
he doesn't steal, doesn't rape. He has honor in his life. Most
important, he knows he's a human being. And he has a victory."

"A victory?"

"Yes. Not too long ago I received a phone call from him.
He had been arrested in another state. He was very agitated.
I asked him why he was so upset, and he told me that he was
charged with assault and robbery. 'I didn't rob the man,' he
told me.

"I spoke with his attorney, told him that I'd post bail and

also be a character witness. The lawyer was shocked. 'Are you sure?' he asked. I told him I was. Well, before I arrived, Allen went before the judge and — on his own — mounted the witness stand and told the truth. He had been sitting in a movie theater, a porno movie theater, and this man sat next to him and fondled him. 'I confess that I hit him,' he told the judge, 'but I did not rob him.' The judge believed Allen, and sentenced him to time served.

"That's a prize, a victory he'll carry all his life. The system actually worked for Allen. He was *believed*. These are my kind of success stories, Walter. I know they're not about scholarships or degrees or awards, but they count."

I knew then that there were some questions I had to ask, questions that would lead me to discover why Andrew Vachss does what he does.

"Were you abused at home as a child?"

"No," he replied. "Quite the contrary. I grew up with a great sense of safety, secure with both my mother and my father. My father would have torn down buildings to protect my brother and me, as would our mother."

"Andrew," I asked, "was there ever a time when you were seriously threatened as a child?"

"You mean beyond the normal fighting among kids on the street?"

"Yes," I said, and I described how, when I was a small boy, an ex-fighter had tried to lure me off the subway.

He sat silently for a couple of seconds, then he leaned forward.

"I've never told anyone this," he began, "but when I was about ten, I was stopped in a vacant lot one afternoon by what I can only describe as a migratory hobo gang, a large group made up of older teenagers and drifters in their twenties. They all lived, as best as I can recall, in an old abandoned building.

" 'We want to show you some really exciting things,' they told me, and they said they had puppies. 'Come with us!' they insisted.

"I was surrounded, trapped. I could not get away. I was frightened, but I was too young to understand this in predatory sexual terms. Months later, a cousin of mine explained what they were really after, but what I sensed in that moment, a vague aura of evil and control, was scary enough. They were passing signals among themselves.

"I remember trying so hard not to tremble — but I trembled anyway.

" 'C'mon!' they told me.

"I started to use the only tools I had, my brain and my mouth. I knew I couldn't fight out of this.

" 'Do I need money?' I asked.

" 'You *got* money?' they asked, extremely interested.

" 'I do at home,' I confided. 'Do I need it?'

" 'Yeah, sure, that's great,' they said. 'Let's get the money.'

"They walked with me to my house. Then they waited across the street. As soon as I got inside, I told my mother what they had said.

"You have to understand about my mother. My father had been a professional football player, a very tough man; my mother could be tougher than he was. I remember once when an enormous man, the father of a bully who had made the mistake of picking on my brother, came to our house screaming and threatening. His son, though he was much larger than my brother, had gotten bloodied. I'm sure he probably lied to his father about the circumstances. Anyway, there was this big man yelling how he was going to give my brother a beating. Quietly, my mother told me to bring her the kitchen knife.

" 'Why do you want that?' the big man asked.

"My mother replied, 'If you come into this house and try

to hurt one of my children, I'm going to plunge this knife into your heart. If you'd like to come back later and discuss all this with my husband, fine. Right now, leave.'

"He left — and he didn't come back.

"Now picture this same woman, my mother, charging down the stairs out onto the street, and the whole hobo gang fleeing! By running, they convinced me they were up to no good. In any case, Walter, the point of this story is, that's as close as I've come to being molested myself, and you can see now why I felt secure even in a hard environment."

"How did you get involved with abused children?"

"I'm asked that so often," he replied, "but I've never really answered it."

He hesitated, his expression serious again.

"Let me try," he said, "*really* try."

"Please," I encouraged him.

"There's really no one thing. Pictures flood my mind. One time, while I was trying to trace a pattern of syphilis in a prison, I found a boy who had gotten rectal gonorrhea from being gang-raped. I remember how I tried to persuade his mother to get him out, that he was in danger.

" 'Let the little faggot die,' she told me.

"That's one image I have," he said, "but that was later in my life."

I sat quietly.

"Walter," he resumed, "when I was a kid, I had a friend with a childhood like yours, a kid whose father beat him. The father was one of those giant bodybuilder-weightlifting types, and he brutalized his son. One day my friend asked me if he could hide in our basement for a while. So I went upstairs with him to ask my father if he could.

" 'Why would he want to do that?' my father asked, but then he looked up, saw the boy's physical condition, and he knew the answer.

" 'No,' my father said, 'he can't stay in the basement. He can stay in your room.'

"The boy was worried. 'My father will come looking for me if he finds out I'm here. It's okay. I can sleep in the basement. No one will know. He won't find me.'

" 'No,' my father reassured him, 'everything will be fine. Sleep in the bedroom, not the basement.'

" 'But my father!' the boy protested.

" 'It will be fine,' my father said again.

"Later, of course, the boy's father came up the block, wearing a muscle-shirt. He was shouting for his son. It was like *High Noon*. He was yelling, cursing, screaming at the top of his lungs, mean as can be. When my father stepped outside, the man demanded, 'Let me have my son!'

"My father said to him, 'You think you're a pretty tough guy, beating up a boy?'

" 'It's my kid. I'll do what I want to.'

" 'Well, try me then.'

"The other boy's father threatened, but it was clear in five seconds that he was only going to bluster. My father waited, not moving. Then the man left — and for the first time, my friend saw this person who had been beating him for what he really was, a lousy bully.

"My father brought my friend back into our home and finished dinner as if nothing had happened. He had risked a lot for that boy, yet he acted as if it were no big deal. Somehow I knew then that my father felt he *had* to help. Maybe that single incident is what started me on this road. Maybe. My parents helped people only because it was right, not for reward. They were willing — they're still willing! — to risk for the right things. Who knows? Maybe, deep down, that's why I do what I do."

"What gives you the most joy?"

"To save a life — because when I save one, I save countless

others. The multiplying effect is incredible. When I stop someone from abusing a child, there's a chance I might be stopping
that child from becoming an abuser. Look, I know there are
people who dream of taking a single dollar and turning it into
a million. My dream's to save a kid — to save the world. Please
don't misunderstand. Mine are not isolated victories. I feel the
joy of winning every day. Some situations are more compelling
and some children are more critical in their need and some
predators are more slimy than others, but each case to me is
important. The joy for me is to win, to do it right, to be
respected for that. I guess I've selected a life for myself in which
I'll never be popular. I accept that. When I hurt some predator,
when I feel wonderful when I've helped jail another — well,
all I can say is that maybe somewhere I have ancestors looking
down at me and smiling because what I'm doing is right, and
I'm doing it to the best of my ability. I don't know if this
answers your question."

"It does, but I have another."

We both laughed.

"Andrew," I asked, "why don't you quit?"

"Because I'm winning," he replied. "I'm an optimist, because
I believe I can save more lives in a year than an emergency
room surgeon. I've seen the results. I've seen young human
beings who would be tomorrow's predators but for the inter-
vention we provide. That, to me, is changing the world. How
could I possibly be a pessimist? I know I can't possibly stop
child abuse by myself — but I can contribute."

"What about pessimists?"

"The pessimist believes he doesn't count. How sad — and
how wrong! By quitting, the pessimist lives his own worst
scenario. Let me say this: If all they'll be able to put on your
tombstone is that your American Express card was paid up,
you may as well not have lived at all. I have no children, by
choice, so what I'll leave behind is what I do. I believe my

work has value. People who laughed at me when I started, ridiculed my hopes and ideals, are already out of the race. They're *gone*. For me, life's a fifteen-round fight. God didn't give me a knockout punch; God didn't give me millions or political power. But if I go the distance and I'm still standing at the end, I'll have ended up with more than all those who started and quit, all those blessed with gifts. I'll make a difference."

I looked closely at my friend, and I knew that this thin, wiry man, his face scarred, his nose broken, his eyepatch askew, lives with more authentic horror, hatred, and tragedy in a day than most of us know all our lives. Yet listening to his voice, crackling and hoarse, I began to understand. Out of a dank well of human squalor and degradation — the world in which Andrew Vachss wages war — hope emerges. If a single flower can bloom in this foul darkness —

"— then you," I said, "have changed the world."

Courage, as I've written elsewhere, is always and only one thing: It is acting *with* fear, not without it. To be brave, we must be afraid. Risk-taking is not easy — and the greatest risk of all is to try to know oneself, and to act on that knowledge. In lives like Andrew's, the commitment is always certain, the solid core that gives people strength. Risk-takers Andrew Vachss, Carol Burnett, Elie Wiesel, Liz Smith, Irving Wallace, Gloria Steinem, Hugh Downs, Phyllis George, Joyce Brothers, Jim Webb, Roger Smith, Olivia de Havilland, W. Clement Stone, Tommy Lasorda, Mimi Silbert, and Norman Vincent Peale are living examples of Elie's perceptive observation: *When our center is strong, everything else is secondary.*

Reflecting on his own life, Norman Vincent Peale said, "When we stand up for something we sincerely believe in, I've found, we can take criticism, even grow from it."

Deep down, what do we most desire?

I want to be somebody.

I remember listening to Jerry Lewis, one of this century's great entertainers and a world-class humanitarian, as he gave the commencement address to the Mercy College graduating class in Dobbs Ferry, New York, in 1987. "It doesn't take much," he told the graduates, "to buy a five-dollar ticket, sit up in the stands at a Tijuana bullring, and yell *Olé!* It takes something more to leap into the arena with the bull. You have to decide for yourself where you'll be. No one can do it for you. . . . Whatever you decide, don't tiptoe. Walk with courage, act with tenacity, and believe me, there's a chance you'll make your goals — and wouldn't that be wonderful? But if you find that you won't be one of the few to make it to the very top, then be courageous in another way: Root with all your heart for those who might."

As he spoke, I recalled how he had once corrected me when I said he was selfless in his lifelong efforts to relieve the suffering of human beings stricken with dystrophic diseases — the people who call themselves Jerry's Kids.

"Walter," he said, "I'm not selfless at all. What I do for the Muscular Dystrophy Association, whether it's the telethons or anything else, I do for *me*. Helping others is the most selfish thing I can do. The joy, the pleasure, I derive from my efforts, the satisfaction, the self-esteem — it is incomprehensible."

Children learn when to trust; adolescents search for identity; adults see beyond themselves.

At no time in my own life were the distinctions that lead to successful risk-taking made more clear to me than when, as an adult, I had to answer a question I had avoided for decades.

One March afternoon in 1987, during a tour of the Soviet Union, I stood with my wife, Loretta, at the edge of a ravine in Kiev, in the Ukraine. It was drizzling and cold. Across the shallow valley I could see gentle birches and firs bend and shift softly, gracefully, in the chill, moist air, their branches dripping wet snow onto the winding, muddy footpaths below. I had seen hundreds of such scenes before, in places like Idaho and New Hampshire and Wisconsin and upstate New York — a familiar landscape of several shades of brown broken by stripes of black and puddles of white; the bark of the trees, as elsewhere, a mottled green and gray, and a dark, mushy mixture of earth and snow melting at their trunks — all signs of the changing season. Yet however familiar these colors, this was a place to which I had never been. This was Babi Yar.

It was here, we were told, that the Nazis who occupied this land on September 29, 1941, had ordered the Jews of Kiev to assemble. "Bring two days' supply of food," the residents were advised — and, of course, "all your valuables." For several days prior to the actual gathering, our guide explained to Loretta and me, the Germans had instigated and encouraged rumors that the Jews would be shipped to Palestine. Thus, instead of the hundreds expected, thousands came, even a handful who were not Jewish at all but fellow Ukrainians posing as Jews, hopeful that they too might escape, might somehow save their babies from this horrible war.

The German soldiers, with the willing assistance of a local militia composed of collaborators, informers, and Nazi sympathizers, quickly stole the food from their captives, seized their possessions, then whipped the now terrified prisoners through a gauntlet. At its end, they ordered the bloodied victims to remove their clothes.

How they must have trembled, I thought, as I stood on the earth at the edge of the ravine where the condemned had stood forty-six years before. Neighbors and strangers humiliated, naked, vulnerable, terror rising in their chests as the killing began;

hidden Nazi machine guns erupting, human beings large and small, ill and infirm, young and old, some still alive, some dead, tumbling into the gulley at my feet; explosive charges tucked into the walls of the small glen detonating, raining dirt heavily onto the bodies — and then, for only a moment, silence, soon broken as the carnage resumed. In two days the Germans executed on this spot 33,771 men, women, and children, because they were Jewish. The Nazi commander received a medal from the Third Reich; no fellow officer, he was told, had killed so many people so quickly.

Although I've studied the English language as a writer and as an editor almost all of my adult life, I can find no word to describe what I felt, standing in the mud at Babi Yar. I can say I felt anger and sorrow and hate and love and pity and loss and regret and I was vengeful, and that would be true, but I felt those emotions all at once, and with them I was empty. I wanted to do *something*, but there was nothing to do.

Loretta spoke before I did.

"What do the Germans say?" she asked the guide.

"Excuse me?"

"Germans visit Babi Yar, don't they?"

"Yes."

"What do the Germans say?"

"If they were old enough to be in the war," the guide replied, "they say they served in Africa."

"Of course," Loretta said, nodding. "What else could they say?"

For a few seconds we stood quietly in the rain.

"Maybe we should leave," suggested the guide, "before we're really soaked."

We hurried to a waiting black Volga, the ubiquitous Soviet automobile. Loretta and I slipped into its back seat, and the driver threaded the car through the downpour, heading across

Kiev to Saint Sophia Cathedral. In the silence I considered how we'd gotten here.

A few weeks earlier I had been invited, as editor of *Parade*, to tour with my wife five cities in the Soviet Union and to arrange a similar tour in the United States for Vitaly Korotich, editor of the popular Soviet magazine *Ogonyok*, and his wife, Zinaida. Both Vitaly and I had agreed — and this was critical to the exchange — to write our impressions of each other's land for articles to appear simultaneously, side by side, in *Parade* and in *Ogonyok*.

My invitation came in a telephone call from Oleg Benyukh, the editor of *Soviet Life* magazine, who was also a deputy to the Soviet ambassador to the United States in Washington.

"Is this possible?" he asked.

"I'll let you know," I said. After speaking with Loretta, I placed a call to Charles Wick, who was director of the United States Information Agency.

"Is this a good idea?" I asked him.

"Yes," he told me. "By all means, this is a *very* good idea. Not only will you be able to decide for yourself whether the Soviets' new policy of openness, what they call *glasnost*, is real and whether it will continue, but even more important, Walter, you'll have an unprecedented opportunity — and responsibility — to write directly to Soviet citizens in their language. I really think you should do this. We'll help you in any way we can."

I told him we'd make the trip.

"Good," he said. "Tell Loretta I guarantee we'll get you out —" he paused "— even if it takes ten years."

"Thanks!" I said, laughing. "That's very reassuring."

Charlie's humor notwithstanding, he was good to his word. His agency, working with Oleg, skillfully arranged all of the necessary visas for our two-week trip to Moscow, Leningrad, Volgograd, Kiev, and Tbilisi, and the USIA staff also helped me to plan the Korotich tour of Washington, D.C., Knoxville, Chicago, New Orleans, and New York.

What I had not anticipated, I reflected quietly as the Volga drove farther away from Babi Yar on that rainy afternoon, was the friendship that was emerging between Vitaly and me; nor had I realized how deeply I'd be affected by this tour, how I'd have to confront a risk that had been buried deep within me for more than thirty years.

The questions had started to tug at me a few days earlier, when, after about an hour's drive from Moscow, we had arrived at Zagorsk, where there is a monastery described to us by Vladimir Alexeev, our translator, as the center of Russian Christianity. "Tourists often come here," Vladimir said.

I was curious. Here, I knew, was a nation that discouraged religion, that treated notions of God as mere myth, that regarded spiritual icons solely as objects of art — a society where atheism was held to be the ideal. I wondered how there could be believers, and if there were, how they learned to believe.

The monastery, I discovered, was a complex of colorful buildings, some five centuries old; one had great blue-and-gold, bulb-shaped towers, others were richly painted with elaborate religious designs, and all were surrounded by a high white wall. One structure, smaller than the others, was the oldest — the Troitskaya Cathedral, built in 1422, on whose walls Andrei Rublev had painted a series of icons, some tracing the Crucifixion of Christ. As we entered this smaller cathedral, which is known in English as the Church of the Trinity, we were joined by a tall young priest named Longin. His beard was a charcoal hue, lush and long, and his large brown eyes were dark as earth. He wore flowing black robes, his hands concealed in their folds.

A rope split the church into distinct halves. On our side

people queued up to kneel before a priest who stood unobtrusively near a far wall. On the other side was, well, an audience, visitors in groups who had come to see a museum. I heard the notes of a hymn in the air — a haunting and penetrating melody, I thought, but one I did not recognize. And where, I wondered, is the choir?

"Longin," I said, "the hymn is wonderful, but I don't see a choir."

He smiled.

"As the people walk through," he explained, "they take up the hymn and it stays on their lips until they leave. The believers are the choir. This choir has new members every day; the singing never stops."

The singers, not surprisingly, were mostly older people, bundled up against the cold with thick woolen coats and mufflers, heavy hats and gloves. Yet when I studied the line more closely, I picked out several small children, a couple in their twenties, three teenage girls, and a teenage boy — and suddenly I was unsettled by the memory of a thirteen-year-old boy, *me*, in a church not much larger than the one in which I was standing, demanding, "If there's a God, strike me dead!"

My eyes started to fill — but not for me, for the moment. I was moved by the conviction of a continuing hymn, the sound of individuals standing tall against the overwhelming tide of their larger society. And I began to sense, maybe for the first time, what I myself believed.

"Longin," I asked as we were leaving, "how did you come to be a priest?"

"At first, like the other children in my village," he told me, "I regarded the stories of the Bible as tall tales. Then — I can't remember precisely when — I started to hear the stories differently. I learned, apart from the other children, to believe, to have faith."

"But that was not what was intended?"

"No," he said. "The stories were told to the children as legends, not to be taken as true."

"Why you?" I asked.

He shook his head.

"Since all the children heard the same stories," he replied, "I don't know why I was chosen by God to have faith, only that I'm truly thankful that I do — and that my life is here."

I considered Longin's answer again as we rode quietly away from Babi Yar. His words had also come to mind earlier in the tour, when we were in Volgograd, the city we visited two days before coming to Kiev. We were told by our guides there that only two buildings had survived World War II, when the city was called Stalingrad. After a long and bitter siege in 1942 and 1943, the Nazis were defeated at Stalingrad. The intensity of the warfare was evidenced by the discovery after the battle that on the plain called Mamayev, where front-line troops had faced each other, more than a thousand shell fragments lay in each square yard of earth — land on which today stands a monument.

It was snowing heavily in Volgograd when we wound our way up a long series of steps to the war memorial, a concrete statue of the Motherland, what the Soviet citizens call Rodina. The statue rose hundreds of feet in the air, her body facing what would have been the march of the invading German army, a sword in her right hand raised high, her head turned back to her people, her left arm extended, imploring them to join her, to fight, to die if they must, her meaning unspoken but clear: *Follow me.* The stark contrasts of this enormous country, this nation of eleven time zones, suddenly seemed to blanket me like the falling snow in a confusing flurry of ideas, starting with the memory of Zagorsk and Longin's extraordinary leap of faith. As we stood in silence, I hoped that in time I'd be better able to sort out the blizzard of images that confounded me, moved me, as we looked up at the tall monument.

Only an hour later we stood in the cold at the entrance to a gray, eight-story, cement-block building on Shemenko Street in the Red Square district, where we were about to have lunch with a poet, Tatiana Baturina, in her flat.

We rode an elevator to her floor, and when she opened the door, she greeted us with a wide smile.

"Welcome!" she said. Then, her English vocabulary exhausted, she immediately looked to Vladimir, our translator, for help.

Our knowledge of Russian was no better.

"Vladimir," I suggested, "it looks like you're going to get to do a lot of talking."

Tatiana, who was forty and slender, had a face, I noticed, like those of many of the models I have known: her features soft and gentle, her eyes large, round, and light brown, her cheeks creamy, unblemished, her hair ebony, shining, short. She wore black corduroy Levis with a pink and maroon feathered blouse, no jewelry, and only faint makeup. Her apartment was large, three or four rooms, and contained polished mahogany units lined with books, some written by her; in her living room there was a color television, and Persian rugs were scattered about.

After a lunch of fresh vegetables, slices of pork, and a chiffon dessert, Tatiana — through Vladimir — started to talk about her work. She'd written seven books of poetry, she said, and had visited Afghanistan, an experience that had so touched her, she had not spoken about it for three months.

"What is it that the poet concerns herself with?" I asked.

Vladimir translated.

"I am dedicated to exploring the life of the soul," she replied.

Her response surprised me. It was not at all what I had expected, but under the circumstances it was compelling.

"Are you a Communist?" I asked.

"Yes," she said.

"Are you an atheist?"

"Yes, of course."

"I'm baffled," I said. "If you do not believe in God, how do you conceive a soul? Perhaps we define the concept in a different way. Can you define *soul* for me?"

She grew agitated and spoke at length with Vladimir, who, flustered, finally told me, "You should have discussed such things at Zagorsk."

"Please don't correct me," I told him. "Ask the questions as I express them. Tatiana is trying to answer."

"It is complicated," she said through Vladimir, "and it is not possible to state simply. Can you?"

To my surprise, I nodded.

"What is the soul?" Vladimir asked.

"Our soul is our essence," I replied — and I realized I had, with no conscious preparation, finally answered for myself the question that had tugged at me for more than thirty years, since the morning I had asked, "Is there a God?" *Now* I understood. I did believe, but not in the same way as the people who sat with me in that Lutheran church so long ago. I was more like Longin; I heard the stories differently.

Vladimir repeated my sentence, and Tatiana became animated.

"More," she encouraged. "Please continue."

I nodded.

"Our soul is the very essence of life," I began, "and denying it does not destroy it. Our soul, this spirit within us, is who we really are. It is what binds us together as human beings and what separates us from all other living things."

"Do *you* believe in God?" Vladimir asked.

"Let me answer with a question," I said. "If a single drop

of water is taken from a raging stream, is the stream forever altered?"

"I don't know," Vladimir replied.

"I think it is," Tatiana said. "What do *you* think?"

Finally, after more than three decades, I could answer with confidence.

"I believe it would be forever altered," I said, "and the stream in which we flow is God. Thus, every life, every soul, has value — and we, unavoidably, are part of each other."

I could not have been aware as I spoke that the very next day I'd be standing at Babi Yar, trying to grasp how one human being could so hurt another. When I watched the birches bend so silently in the rain at Babi Yar, I thought, this is a horrible place of death.

"And of hope," I was told by Vitaly Korotich three days later, when we returned to Moscow.

"Hope?" I asked, puzzled.

We were sitting in the editor's elegant home, an apartment more modern and larger than most of those we had visited. It was decorated warmly with paintings, including a large oil portrait of Vitaly by the world-renowned Soviet artist Ilya Glazunov; the den was filled with posters, mementos from around the world, fine furniture in soft leathers and bright fabric and hand-rubbed woods arranged with care in front of long shelves enclosed in glass and neatly stacked with hundreds of volumes, many in English, a language in which the editor of *Ogonyok* magazine was fluent. His sons, Vitaly Jr., who was fifteen, and Nikita, who was eleven, joined us for dinner, and their father, an engaging host, poured sweet red Ukrainian wine and frozen vodka from Kiev. Meanwhile, beneath a crystal chandelier in the dining room, their mother generously spread out an exquisite meal of varied meats and vegetables, caviar, fresh fruit, a platter of light chocolate candies and sweet custard-filled pastries — more food, I calculated, than a group twice our size could eat.

"*Hope?*" I repeated, quietly bewildered, my body at this table of plenty, my mind focused elsewhere.

Our host nodded.

"I will tell you a story about Babi Yar," he said, "a true story you have not heard before."

At fifty-one, Vitaly Korotich was eight years older than I, and he was, I knew, a native of Kiev. His face was round and open, his cheeks pink and warm, his brown eyes wide and bright as he spoke. His eyebrows arched continually in good humor. His clothes were casual — a blue and red velour sweater over a white cotton shirt. I knew that this friendly man, my modest host, at ease and unassuming, was a poet and author of considerable intellect — and courage. He had trained as a doctor at the Medical Institute in Kiev and had earned a gold medal as class valedictorian. In 1965, though, at the age of twenty-nine, he gave up medicine "to be, finally, what I knew in my heart I had to be," he said — to work full-time as a writer — and in that year he was elected secretary of the Ukrainian Writers' Union. Later he edited a Ukrainian magazine, *Ranok*, and wrote free-lance, and he eventually published more than forty books in fifteen languages. He was honored with the Ukrainian and all-Soviet state poetry prizes, recognized by the International Organization of Journalists, and named an honorary cultural figure in Poland for his translations of Polish poetry.

Remarkable as these achievements were, I thought they paled beside his accomplishment with *Ogonyok*, of which Vitaly had become editor only a year before our dinner. In a series of bold and dramatic moves (which he repeatedly called "normal"), he published several provocative and critical articles previously banned by the authorities, and, stretching the limits of *glasnost*, introduced investigative reporting to the Soviet press. Quickly *Ogonyok* became the Soviet Union's most eagerly sought publication (although not without its editor emerging at the center of a political hurricane), and the magazine's 1.5 million copies continued to be whisked off newsstands, sold out within an hour.

"I was a boy in Kiev." Vitaly started to speak, beginning the story that would lead back to Babi Yar. His tone was no longer light but somber, even dark. "I was barely six years old when the Nazis came, in 1941. Sometimes a German would bathe himself naked in the street, and the Ukrainian men, women, and children would look away, pretending they didn't see. War was my childhood — and children were not safe. We knew that if a German was sleeping in someone's home and a baby cried, he might wake up, shoot the baby if it annoyed him, and return to sleep, *soundly*, bothered no more than if he had killed a fly. To most Nazis, we were not people. They didn't see us; they saw through us.

"When the Gestapo arrested my father and took him away, my mother tried to follow him. Then *she* was gone. I was six, alone. I had no choice but to try to find my parents. By myself I traveled two hundred miles during the war. It took me a year to reach my mother, and she told me she had located the place where the Gestapo had taken my father, and he was still alive. I was seven at the end of this journey, and I had walked, mostly, and I had had to ask for food along the way. Often people without very much themselves shared whatever bits of food they had with me; others took what little *I* had. And I kept walking.

"In war you learn about people, and not always what you might expect. One morning, unthinking, I ran between two buildings into what children always tried to avoid, a group of German soldiers. When a soldier signaled me to come to him,

I had to obey. Then he reached slowly into his jacket. He's going to take out a pistol, I thought, my heart racing, but when he withdrew his hand, he held a harmonica, and there were tears in his eyes. He stretched out his hand, his fingers opened — and he nodded to me. I took the harmonica, and then he smiled. I've often wondered whether I reminded that young soldier of someone he knew, a son somewhere in Germany, a little brother perhaps. So, Walter, I remember the killing — far too much and too terrible for me to be able to describe — but you must know there was a harmonica also. And so it was with Babi Yar."

"The hope you talked about?" I interrupted.

"Yes," he replied.

"Please tell me."

"The Nazis," he said, "started with the mass murders in those first two days, which you know about."

I nodded.

"But it did not stop there. The Germans executed more Jews, then Communists, prisoners of war, *anyone*. By war's end, hundreds of thousands of people had been murdered at Babi Yar, their bodies heaped in piles under the dirt." He paused.

"And then the Nazis became concerned for themselves. The Battle of Stalingrad did not go well for them, and elsewhere their losses were mounting. Faced with the prospect of defeat, the Nazis worried that their horrible crimes would be discovered and that they'd have to account for them. So they tried to destroy the evidence of their terrible deeds. Before the war ended, the German soldiers forced the Jewish prisoners who were still alive to exhume, then burn, the bodies of those who were dead. The stench of so many decomposing corpses was unbearable, and many of the prisoners were able to work only for an hour or so. Kiev, I remember, was in smog, a heavy, thick, stinking smog from the burning of the bodies. It was *terrible*." He paused again.

"But in this nightmare there emerged a great lesson, one I could not document until many years after. You see, some of the victims had hoped to the end that they'd be saved — others simply could not grasp what was happening — and tucked in their undergarments or elsewhere on their person were the keys to their flats — as if they would be able to return! The prisoners who had to burn the bodies searched for these keys and concealed them in their own clothes. Late at night, they quietly tried each key to see if any opened the lock to the barracks in which they were imprisoned. One night, one worked. Hundreds fled. Most, of course, were cut down by the guards' machine guns. Fifteen made it, though, and six of those are still alive — five in the Soviet Union and one in Israel. Many years after their escape, I found and interviewed the survivors for a movie I was making at the time."

"And the lesson?" I asked.

"The keys to save us all," he said, "are in the pockets of the dead."

"Thank you," I said, and I asked no further questions about Babi Yar. I understood that in the story Vitaly had shared, he had found hope, the promise of a future amid despair.

A few minutes later, though, after his sons had left us alone in the den, I reminded my host of an observation told to me by his friend, the artist Ilya Glazunov.

"In your country," Ilya had said, "intellectual disagreements are of the mind, but here they are written in blood. Vitaly, who is like a brother to me, is at risk."

I asked Vitaly, "If Ilya is correct and there are those here who would kill you for what you publish, then why do you take these risks?"

"For the same reasons," he said, "that a person would take such risks in America — for what I really believe in, for something better for Vitaly and Nikita and their children. Because I've known war, I want peace. What I want, Walter, is *normal*."

Later, in the Sovietskaya Hotel, where we were staying in Moscow, I had trouble sleeping. Tomorrow, I thought, will be my last full day in the Soviet Union; this tour's over. Still, though — and this is what troubled me — I had one more invitation. In the morning I was to meet with some of the leaders of Novosti, the Soviet press agency, and I'd be asked to speak. I worried: What am I going to say?

The harder I tried to think, the more confused I became. I turned, fidgeted in bed, arose, walked into the living room, pulled back the drapes to a large bank of windows, and looked into the cold Moscow night. What, I wondered, am I going to say?

Images of the past two weeks burst in my mind, like bubbles in a boiling kettle. When I tried to hold one, though — *this is what I'll talk about!* — instantly it would evaporate, only to be replaced by another: Longin; the church in Zagorsk; a hundred war memorials; a small boy named Ilya on holiday in Volgograd; a family of actors at home in Kiev singing a haunting Ukrainian melody; Loretta playing with their two-year-old daughter, Dasha; morning lines to see the Wyeth family art exhibit in Leningrad; afternoon lines to buy vodka in Moscow; longer lines to see Lenin's tomb; *Sleeping Beauty* delicately performed by the Kirov Ballet in Leningrad; the majesty of that city's Hermitage museum; the precious art; a Rublev icon restored by craftsmen under the leadership of the brilliant Mikhail Deviatoft at the Repin Institute; the black swastika that remained, stamped on its back half a century earlier by some anonymous Nazi; four elderly men who offered me a matzoh at a synagogue in Tbilisi, Soviet Georgia; later, in the same town, anti-Semitic jokes — this last contrasting sharply with the inviting hospitality of Vitaly and Zinaida, the lively and sensitive discussion about human development I held with some eminent professors of the Soviet Academy of Pedagogical

Sciences, and the enthusiasm of a group of scientists for the Volgograd Polytechnic Institute, their distinguished university, which had risen from the rubble of Stalingrad; the tense moment in Moscow when I had interrupted the Soviet minister of education, in front of his subordinates, in the midst of a barrage of criticism he had begun to volunteer about my country.

"Mr. Yagodin," I said, "you and I can spend the next half hour with you telling me about Vietnam and Grenada and Nicaragua and with me reminding you about Hungary and Czechoslovakia and Afghanistan. At the conclusion of this discussion, both of us will be more annoyed and less convinced that we are right now. However, if you'd like to continue, I assure you I'm fully prepared."

He changed the subject.

I'd rather not have another unpleasant exchange, I told myself, but nevertheless, if I have to . . . *What am I going to say?*

Finally, a few minutes after 4:00 A.M., the fog started to evaporate; the risk was clear. I could minimize the opportunity, play it safe, challenge no one, shake hands and go home. Or I could try to say what I really felt, which would be to risk failing to find the right words and thus to embarrass myself, my magazine, and, unintentionally and by association, my country. After all, I thought, I'm no diplomat; I'm an editor — and a guest. I don't have to say a thing, and if I'm silent, who would ever know? Who cares what I say, anyway? If, on the other hand, I don't seize the opportunity to be heard . . .

I found my answer: *I* would know. *I* care. I *had* to try.

"Do you know what you're going to say?" Loretta asked when she arose.

"I think so," I said.

A few hours later we sat in the spacious mahogany-paneled office of Novosti's first deputy chairman of the board, Sergei

Ivanko. He faced me across a long conference table; to his left sat George Fediashin, the vice president and director of news, and at his side sat Boris Karlov, the leader of the North American department of Novosti. Loretta sat on my right, and next to her was Vladimir Alexeev, the Novosti editor who, throughout the tour, had been our translator — but Sergei Ivanko, I realized quickly, needed no interpreter.

"We hope you enjoyed our country," he said, "and I trust that you have received all that you have requested."

"We have," I said, "and thank you."

The room went silent; it was an awkward pause.

"I assume you have some interest in my impressions of your country," I volunteered, breaking the silence.

"Yes," Sergei replied quickly, "we do."

"Then let me start," I said. "First, though, let me say that I'm aware that Charles Wick told you of my government's interest in this trip."

"Yes," Sergei confirmed.

"Then please understand that what I'm about to say is only what *I* feel. I speak not for my government or for my fellow citizens, but for me. My words are mine alone."

"We understand," Sergei said.

Again, silence.

"No one," I began, "can walk among your people, travel through five cities in two weeks, and really know you. You are too much like the people of my own country to be known that easily — a shell within a shell, like your toy dolls, each layer concealing another, more interesting layer, then another. I was welcomed into your homes, schools, theaters, museums, religious places, government agencies — but I am an American, am I not? I see with the eyes of an American.

"What is it that I see? Two symbols come to mind. The first is one of great patriotism, Rodina. She is in your earth and in your very souls. I saw her face in the great statue at Volgograd and I saw her in the face of a schoolgirl in Tbilisi. Again I saw her in a portrait of Visotsky in Leningrad and in an unfinished painting of Pushkin. I heard her voice when a Moscow poet spoke, and when an actor and an actress in Kiev sang after dinner in their home, and when one of your filmmakers in Georgia enthusiastically shared his work with me, and when a nine-year-old boy sought to practice his English with my wife during an intermission of the Kirov Ballet.

"The second symbol I see is one of love, and that would be of a grandparent holding the hand of a grandchild. Nowhere, not on any street in any small village or in any large city, did I see a child unattended. Even your schools for small children are impressive. What hope for the future! Your love of family — the strength of your commitment to each other — is inspiring.

"But there is more. War permeates the very air you breathe. Its remnants, its scent, its reminders are everywhere. Twenty million of your citizens died in the last world war. No family was unaffected. Thus, I recognize that no one can come here and talk to you about war; you know war in an intimate way. Yet I too have known war. For most, if not all, of the people I've spoken with during this tour, I was the first Vietnam veteran that they had ever met. And I'm convinced that these individuals do not want war — and they do not want it with a passion and in a way that is profoundly personal. But it is equally clear to me that your leaders have tried to prepare you for war. Even as we speak, your brothers, sons, fathers die in Afghanistan.

"Hence your propaganda, some of which starts right in this room. All arguing aside, you know in your hearts you have not told the truth about my country. You may want to respond that America has propagandized too. And I would have to agree. But should you and I stop there? You can see, there are no scales on my eyes. I know there are basic, fundamental differences between our societies, but maybe each of us can find some wisdom in the old preacher's sermon: What binds us together on this earth as human beings is greater than what separates us.

"Thus, I'd like to help you to understand Americans, certainly not all but at least one — me. I am descended from anonymous ancestors who could have been poor people seeking riches or zealots in a noble cause or rabblerousers fleeing some mischief, or worse. I really don't know who my people were further back than a generation or two. Like so many of my countrymen, I am a mongrel. We too have a statue, in New York Harbor, and she calls to people like me, patchwork ancestry and all. I have a bias, a deep, unyielding bias, in favor of the guiding principles upon which my own nation has been founded. This, I know, does not surprise you.

"Why do I tell you what you already know? Because I want to trust you — and I assume you want to trust me. Well, if this is true, then you need to understand Americans a little better — the real us, not the propaganda that has been spread too thick, too long. As I said, I speak for me — and there are certain beliefs I have as an American that I cannot compromise. After remarks I've made in various places during the past few days, I'm quite certain you know it's important to me that Jews be allowed to leave the Soviet Union. It is even more important to understand, though, that I would feel the same if the freedom of passage were denied to Christians, Muslims, or for that matter atheists.

"Who am I to come to your country and say such things? Again, I have no scales on my eyes. I know that the settlers of my nation slaughtered Indians, that human slavery was endorsed by the founders in our Constitution. I'm aware that during World War II my country imprisoned loyal Americans because their parents happened to be Japanese, and that only after that war were black soldiers and white soldiers allowed to sleep in the same barracks. I realize that it wasn't until 1954 that our schools were required to be integrated — a momentous decision that took marches, demonstrations, government troops, and years to enforce. Worse, I know that racial prejudice, though no longer the law of the land, continues to trouble — and weaken — my country. So who am I to talk to you about Jews?

"I am a friend who says: What is wrong is wrong. I know that prejudice here is no less evil than any that exists in my own country, and like all hatred, it is self-destructive. Indeed, it is the foolish Soviet citizen who finds relief in the knowledge that there may be men and women in America who harbor similar hatreds.

"As I see it, our goal should not be to see how small we can be or how many people we can hurt. Rather, how many can we help? What can we do together to improve the lot of human beings on earth? Thus, what I ask, I ask out of love: Have not enough Jews been hurt? Must we war over this issue? I pray it does not have to come to that. But I cannot be sure it will not. And I know, as you do, that if we fight, our two nations will leave an earth so scorched that even Babi Yar would pale.

"The first step for each of us is trust. Your great nation has risen from the crumbled ruins of war in less than half a century; it has clothed, educated, housed its people. Intolerance? Surely you are better than that. *We* are better than that.

"I have told you what I sincerely believe. Now I thank you for your patience, your courtesy, your hospitality, your candor, your generosity. And your warmth. I hope you feel we've responded in kind. This has been a wonderful visit, and I feel I have made friends. I hope you agree. I wish you could understand how deeply I have been affected by this visit. Maybe someday you will. In the meantime, for all of us a question remains. Maybe we can at least begin to answer it this morning: Will we wage war, or will we wage peace? I am for peace."

Sergei Ivanko, who had not once dropped his eyes as I spoke, reached across the table and clasped my hand.

"So am I," he said.

I had spoken for forty minutes; I had said precisely what I wanted to say.

Conclusion

Throughout this book I've used the editorial *we* whenever possible, because, as I suggested in the introduction, this is a journey we needed to take together. In a few minutes, though, you'll turn the last of these pages, and your life will continue to be what it has been — yours alone. I hope the voices you've heard here stay with you, accompany you, return to your consciousness when you most need them — and I hope they've helped you to understand that you need no tidy formulas to face risks, that the principles we've shared are sound and sustaining, that you *can* learn to master the process of risk-taking, that you *can* find within yourself the noble motives to realize your dreams.

I've challenged some popular notions here, particularly regarding our entry into adulthood, because I believe that when we are adolescents we are encouraged to internalize a calendar that causes undue distress, disappointment, even tragedy.

What is the *right* age? Sometimes it seems to me that we're given a report card, and our grades are dependent on a point in time: "I married late; I married early." How often do we ask, am I doing okay for my age? Am I too young? Or am I too old? This, in a century when people are thriving in their eighties, when life expectancy continually increases. When *is* middle age? Forty, sixty, seventy-five?

Chronological age, a yardstick across a stream, is a flimsy guide to our health, to our career status, to most of our real needs. How emotionally secure is the twenty-nine-year-old who has taken risk upon risk to become a vice president and who is now depressed because she won't be president by thirty? How adult is the widower who first risks marrying a younger woman, then refuses to risk having the child they both want because he worries about how it will look?

My point is not to deny that the timing of crucial events in our lives is important. Quite the contrary. If your mother dies when you're seven, undoubtedly the impact is greater than if she dies when you're thirty-seven. And if the impact somehow *were* the same, would you, despite your actual age, be a child, an adolescent, or an adult? Often crises occur — risk is thrust upon us — when life events don't match the calendar we've come to accept.

Children learn when to trust; adolescents search for identity; *adults see beyond themselves.*

Be assured, it's not possible for human beings to be empty vessels. No person who has ever lived has been an unbeliever, despite what they may argue. Everyone believes in something. It might be God or no God, manifest greed for money or power, a career or a friend, science, a principle — *something.* Whatever it is we place before ourselves is what we run toward. A story told to me by a friend, Father Joseph Kelly, might be useful. It's about a young priest who began to doubt his vocation.

One afternoon in the dead of winter, he passed a small boy — homeless, skinny, his jacket threadbare, his tiny body huddled over a street grate as he tried to absorb the heat from the subway tunnel below.

"God!" the priest exclaimed, his frustration at a boil. He looked back at the shivering child. "God," he demanded, "why do you allow this? Why don't you do something about it? Don't you give a damn?"

In his mind, to his astonishment, he heard for the first time what he knew was the voice of his Lord:

"I do care," he was told, "and I have done something about it. I created *you*."

Choose what you believe.

Your life is yours alone — and to live it as an adult is to accept that no single risk can solve all of your problems, achieve all of your dreams, or even be enough. To want to be more than we are is real and normal and healthy — and adults respect the process.

Define a clear goal.

Review the positive, practical, and potential losses.

Identify elements of trust, identity, larger purpose.

Ask, am I responding as a child, as an adolescent, as an adult? Take only the risks you intend to take; beware of hidden agendas. Risks taken because we're hurt or angry or jealous are usually unwise and unrewarding, whatever their outcome.

Watch your timing. But don't use that legitimate concern as an excuse to hesitate.

Act.

I believe the risks worth taking are those that lead to the most fulfilling life. When we commit to high ideals, we succeed *before* the outcome is known.

Your life is worth a noble motive.

Acknowledgments

When I first told Alex Haley, the acclaimed author of *Roots*, that I planned to write a book exploring how we can learn to take risks, he encouraged me: "Nothing is more important. Too often we are taught how *not* to take risks. When we are children in school, for example, we are told to respect our heroes, our founders, the great people of our past. We are directed to their portraits hanging on walls and in hallways and reproduced in textbooks. What we are not told is that these leaders, who look so serene and secure in those portraits, were in fact rule-*breakers*. They were risk-takers in the best sense of the word; they dared to be different."

Now, having written *The Greatest Risk of All*, I understand even more clearly Alex's perceptive observation and my debt to the remarkable people who have shared their time and their stories with me.

Also, I would like to express my deep thanks to the many others who have helped me: my wife, Loretta, who has been the first editor of all that I have written and whose steadfast love and support are the strongest pillars of my life; my son, Eric, and my daughter, Melinda, for having the patience and the sensitivity to encourage their dad; my distinguished editor, Marc Jaffe, whose ideas were so eloquently expressed, whose

241

insights were so wisely shared, and whose enthusiastic support so markedly improved this work.

I was inspired throughout this journey by Jack Scovil of the Scott Meredith Literary Agency, who's there when I need him most; by Gillian Holzhauser, a colleague who lives with great courage; by my assistant, Gida Ingrassia, who makes me seem better than I am.

I'm especially grateful to Si Newhouse, whose friendship and counsel I cherish; to Liz Duvall at Houghton Mifflin for her sharp eye and wise suggestions; to Carlo Vittorini, *Parade* publisher; to my friends Peachy and Manny Santos, Susan Kesselman, Wilbert LeMelle, Lloyd Jones, Sal Didato, Wallace and Carolyn Wolf, Barbara Gordon, Clay Felker, Jhoon Rhee (a teacher who says yes to life), Marguerite Michaels, Barbara Goldsmith, David Starr, and *Jersey Journal* editor Steve Newhouse; to Catherine Hemlepp; and to the editors, authors, photographers, and artists of *Parade*, with whom I work and who continue to encourage me — Diane Ackerman, Eddie Adams, Cleveland Amory, Jack Anderson, Donna Arcieri, Chris Austopchuk, Stuart Berger, Lisa Birnbach, James Brady, Sara Brzowsky, Jacqueline Burns, Fran Carpentier, Sey Chassler, Jane Ciabattari, Haskell Cohen, Bob Colacello, David Currier, Ovid Demaris, Joseph DiBlasi, John Frook, Roberta Gardner, Bernard Gavzer, Elizabeth Gaynor, Opal Ginn, Anita Goss, David Halberstam, David Hegeman, Ron Hillery, Bill and Bunny Hoest, Joy Jackson-Childs, Renee Keller, Herbert Kupferberg, Larry L. King, Elinor Klein, Aaron Leonard, Sheila Lukins, Peter Maas, Norman Mailer, Milagros Maldonado, Gael McCarthy, Lynn Minton, Linda Mohler, Willie Morris, Robert Nisonoff, Michael O'Shea, Beverly Pabarue, Brent Petersen, Teressa Platt, Arlene Pueschel, Dotson Rader, Mary Rose, Julee Rosso, Michael Ryan, Carl Sagan, Bonnie St. Clair, Al Santoli, Dick Schaap, Marvin Scott, Tom Seligson, Lloyd

Shearer, Gail Sheehy, Larry Smith, Tad Szulc, Martin Timins, Al Troiani, John Twomey, Earl Ubell, Michael VerMeulen, Marilyn vos Savant, Lally Weymouth, Miriam White, Hank Whittemore, Patricia Wolf, Linda Wong, Bridgette Wright, and Ira Yoffe.

Of course, there would be no book without my mother, Ethel D'Ambra, the courageous lady I love and admire so dearly, and my stepfather, Gene D'Ambra, whose kindness, generosity, and gentleness brighten the world.

And my special thanks to the Becktoft, Thiele, and Artz families — my aunts, uncles, and cousins — and to my brother, Bill, who knows about risk.